MAINLINES IN MODEST SPACES

If you must have grand trains, you'll need a big layout. And trains don't
come much grander than the 'Cornish Riviera Express', here climbing
Dainton behind 6001 'King Edward VII' in 1937.

MAINLINES IN MODEST SPACES

Iain Rice

ATLANTIC PUBLISHERS

Front Cover -

Main Picture: Modest mainline train; the Southern in North Cornwall.

Lower Left: Torreyford; main line icon.

Lower Right: Rawnook - a pre-group theme in EM.

Rear Cover -

Bursting under the bridge in a cloud of steam - a 'Sonay' on an East Suffolk train.

Atlantic Publishers

Trevithick House, West End, Penryn,
Cornwall TR10 8HE

ISBN: 1-902827-11-2

British Cataloguing in Publication Data
A catalogue for this book is available from the British Library

Printed by Marshalls Offset Printing Ltd., London

Contents

MODEL RAILWAYS
Atlantic
HANDBOOK SERIES Volume 2

Introduction

Like many an active railway modeller of today, I was fortunate enough to grow up in the 1950s and 1960s. So I got to know the railways in that glorious era, the swansong of steam and the dawn of the diesel age. As a spotty, short-trousered schoolboy, I (together with a veritable hoarde of my contemporaries) spent quite a lot of my spare time just watching the trains go by. It was the greatest free show on Earth.

I was never that keen a number-collector - much too clerical and organised for me. No, what I loved above all was the sheer drama of the railway - and nowhere was that drama more apparent than on the main lines. Much though I loved our local lines in East Anglia, I lusted after grander (and much faster) routes than these for my regular 'fix'. Which meant lashing out six bob (nearly two weeks' pocket money!) on a Green Rover bus ticket or - later - climbing aboard the trusty Rudge and pedalling off westwards. The destination? Welwyn, Hadley Wood, Potters Bar - anywhere acccessible on the GN main line, that thoroughbred racetrack of a railway, where the mellow chime of an A4 streaking southwards would make the hairs on the back of your neck stand up!

I got to know other main lines and other excitements - the scream of a sparkling Britannia bearing down on Diss at eighty-plus with a Norwich express, the four-cylinder purr of a Duchess gliding up through Harrow (where my cousins lived), the glint and glamour of the Great Western forging westwards out of London. I saw Gresley engines labouring skyward over the Waverly route, and odd mixtures of ancient 4-4-0s and space-age Bullied streamliners toiling up to Masbury on the S & D. And later - in the early 1960s, in my teens, I was dispatched westward for holidays in distant, magic North Cornwall. We went by the wonderful 'Atlantic Coast Express', me ostensibly in charge of one or two of my siblings while our parents, the dogs, mountains of luggage and the younger Rices perspired down the A30 in the family Morris.

It was in Cornwall that I passed some of my happiest lineside hours. I would leave the rest of them to their boring beaches and worthy walks, and bus or bicycle off in search of trains. To Wadebridge, Boscarne or Dunmere on the Southern or - best of all - Bodmin Road on the Great Western. Here was surely Shangri-La! The beauty of the setting - the woods steep-to at the lineside, the blazing banks of Rhododendrons, the narrow lane that pierced the long, curving embankment, and the cool clear stream that ran beside it - was joy enough. Add a summer Saturday parade of trains - Counties, Halls, Granges, Moguls, and Castles on the main with, as an entre-act, the fussy comings and goings on the steep-graded branchline up to mysterious Bodmin - and one had Paradise. Is this the perfect prototype?

I've never had the space for a proper main-line model railway - the nearest I get is my 12 x 3ft Hornby-Dublo lay-out, where at least A4s, Duchesses and Castles can race by in a deafening roar of tinplate (even if they are pulling about 4G on the curves!) So the plans and musings presented here are a mix of nostalgia and pragmatism that I hope those of you less spacially challenged than I will find useful.

Iain Rice
Chagford, Devon. Autumn 2003

CHAPTER 1

The Main Line as a Subject

I don't know about you, but I started off my model railway career with a main line layout. Most of us did, back then - if we were lucky, and the lusted-after 'Flying Scotsman' or 'Royal Scot' trainset finally arrived one Christmas morning. The object of my particular cravings was a Dublo 'Sir Nigel Gresley' set, with the teak articulated coaches. Alas, in the straightened circumstances of the times (we're talking 1952 here), that was a bit like today's youth hoping for a first date with Britney Spears; reality was a Rovex 'Princess Elizabeth', two 'shorty' coaches and an oval of chunky grey-based 'Series 1' track - 27s 6d the lot at Marks and Spencer's. As with many a dream, mere reality was a poor substitute. The plain black 'Princess' with its drab maroon coaches, lack of valve gear, distorted proportions and crude 'mushroom'

pick-ups below the cab somehow encapsulated the austerity of the day. It in no way compared with the gloss and glamour of a Binns Road 'Streak' - all garter blue paint, red wheels, flashing bright-metal siderods and gorgeous gold-and-white carriages.

The 'Princess' worked off a battery via a black control box with a red plastic knob. It ran like a thing possessed for about the first ten minutes, like a lame duck for the next several days, and gave up the ghost within a week. Within a month or two it had curled up like a stale cheese sandwich, while the maroon coaches faded rapidly to a dull, unappetising pink (reminiscent of that indeterminate blancmange you used to get for school dinners) and sagged in the middle. I did acquire a pair of points and a few wagons, and soon I had given up

The main line layout par excellence - Torreyford, on Ken Northwood's North Devonshire.
This was what it was all about.
Author's Collection.

Torreyford again. Whatever its faults to modern eyes, it has main line atmosphere in spadefuls.
Author's Collection.

Main line layouts are about more than just passenger trains.
Author's Collection.

the main line oval in favour of a bit of plain track and couple of long, wandering sidings. The tender of the 'Princess' became a push-along diesel, and I embarked on my first 'shunting layout'. I've been building them ever since.

That's not to say that I never had any interest in express trains or wanted a main line layout. I did - I've just never been lucky enough to have either the space or the appropriate ingredients to build one of my own. In spite of one or two short-lived attempts to replicate bits of the Southern's main line to the West, that has been the status quo ever since. I've had to do my main line modelling in 3-rail Dublo or at a remove, by getting involved in other people's projects. Which wasn't such a bad idea as, among other lessons, it taught me that large, complex main line layouts are not always the joy for ever they might seem. Indeed, quite a few of them were more by way of a millstone around the owner's neck!

Main line modelling: a brief history

Back in the truly spacious days of railway modelling, when Captain Fleetwood-Shaw and the Rev. Edward Beal held sway, the main line as a subject was taken for granted and executed on the grand scale. Quadruple track? Station platforms long enough to take a twelve-coach train? A ten-platform terminus? A decent run between stations? No problem. At least, not if you were sufficiently well-heeled and lived in the right sort of grand house. Which was usually one with extensive attics or cellars, or some convenient outbuildings - a coach-house or two, that sort of thing - in which to house a monster layout. Many of the large main line model railways of these earlier days

were conceived and executed in just such circumstances, by men who were also able to command the services of some very skilled craftsmen to bring their models into being. The results were often outstanding; layouts like the famous Norris fine scale O gauge empire would stand comparison with anything produced since, while something along the lines of Theo Pearson's expansive 00 gauge 'North Midland' was what main line modelling was all about. It was the sort of layout every schoolboy lusted after.

Before setting out to pen one of these chatty little essays I spend a fair bit of time reading back through my collection of model railway magazines, which goes back to around 1935. This is always an educational experience, whether in the appreciation of Maskelyne's erudition and polished prose or Ahern's wit, wonder at the meticulous skill of modellers such as Alex Jackson and Stan Garlick, or astonishment at the detailed prototype knowledge of people like the late Mike Longridge. Apart from reinforcing the realisation that very little is new under the sun, it's also fascinating for the insight it gives into the social history of railway modelling, as the pattern that emerges is one of a gradual downward spread of the hobby through society - and with it, a change of emphasis and subject.

A number of developments had an important influence on this trend, a trend which has progressively moved the focus away from the grand main line layout toward the humbler (for which read 'branchline') subjects more commonly tackled in these egalitarian days. I suppose the first key influence was Frank Hornby, who set out to make model trains for a much

Curves are both a problem and an asset on a model railway. One thing is certain, however - trains on curves look good.
This, of course, is the GWR in South Devon, hugging the coast between Dawlish and Teignmouth, prior to 1910.
Author' Collection.

broader market than was catered for by traditional 'bespoke' firms like Basset-Lowke or Edward Exeley. Hornby 0-gauge and later, Hornby-Dublo, brought good quality models within the reach of many more people, and Hornby's early championing of 00 gauge (a bold move in 1937, surely?) addressed the lack of space available for model railways in more modest homes. Mainline modelling for the masses became possible.

After the war, Hornby's boldness paid off, and the middle classes took to the model railway hobby in droves when they realised that 00 not only worked well, but could capture the dash and glamour of the traditional steam-hauled express train in the context of a normal suburban semi. This change was reflected in the model railway press of the early 1950s, where 00 gauge began its rapid eclipse of the 0 gauge or larger sizes that had largely featured before the war. In 1950, Lines Bros. moved into the 00 market, offering lower-priced products under the Rovex/Triang brand - model trains with an even wider potential appeal. Support for the smaller scale from specialist firms also grew apace, while writers like Cyril

Freezer and Jack Shortland began to point out the modelling potential of branch lines and other non-main-line subjects for space-starved modellers. The sun rose on the Great Western branchline terminus while the main-line-themed layout gradually lost its long-held status as the 'automatic first choice'.

The possibilities of the smaller scales

Some modellers, however, also saw the possibilities of the combination of the new smaller scale models with a traditional larger site to create a far more realistic style of main line layout, one which represented an actual prototype 'in the round'. Some very ambitious projects got under way at this time, the most memorable of which was probably Ken Northwood's 'North Devonshire', a layout destined to have a life of half a century and which became an icon for a whole generation - mine! The important difference between the Northwood style of mainline layout and latter-day 'grand' affairs like, for instance, Jim Russell's 'Little Western' was that they were, essentially, exercises in D-I-Y. Where Russell and the other members of the 'gentleman's school' commissioned their models from the likes of Roche or Fourmillaid,, Northwood & Co adapted mass-market RTR or built things themselves.

Several other very influential and long-lived 4mm scale 'main line' layouts had their genesis at much the same time, of which the most enduring is without doubt the Rev. Peter Denny's 'Buckingham Branch', closely followed by Frank Dyer's 'Borchester', D A Williams EM 'Metropolitan Junction' and M A Randall's 'Crewminster'. 'Buckingham' may have started out as a simple country branchline, but it soon acquired at least 'secondary mainline' status - Grandborough Junction is a textbook example of successful main line modelling in a modest space, while Buckingham itself eventually became Marylebone in all but name. 'Borchester' showed that an apt choice of prototype (a secondary route in the Nottinghamshire coalfields) also allowed the creation of a 'main line' feel in a surprisingly small space - in portable form to boot - while 'Metropolitan Junction' and 'Crewminster' were both bedroom-sized home layouts that could handle plausible express trains, for all their compromises of site and size.

With the advent of good-quality N scale in the later 1970s, further new avenues of mainline modelling were opened up. The Model Railway Club's 'Chiltern Green' showed what was possible, and led to the current generation of 2mm scale main-line masterpieces: Copenhagen Fields, Chee Tor and Acton Main Line, to pick only three well-known on the exhibition circuit. The ready availability, excellent running quality and relatively modest spatial requirements of modern N offer considerable scope for modelling a variety of main line subjects even in a constrained domestic environment.

What makes a mainline main?

"Define your terms!" my old science master would below at me, as I launched off into the usual halting exposition of Boyle's law or some other scintillating bit of half-understood science. It's a good rule, I find, that helps keep the thought processes on track. So what is a main line, and how does it differ - at least in terms of what we need to model - from lesser railways?

This is a question that can be considered from several angles. Logic says - correctly - that a main line is a section of railway connecting together places of importance. Or, put another way, it is a route which, by the nature of the points it connects, produces enough traffic to justify and support a linking service. In terms of the great trunk routes of the British railway system - the East and West coast lines to the north and Scotland, the Midland striking through the heart of the country, and the Great Western reaching out for Bristol, the West Country and Wales - this is self-evident. It's a bit less clear on, say, the 'Brighton' where - quadruple track notwithstanding - all the trains are EMUs of one sort or another, and none of them goes any great distance.

Of course, being a spotty little London schoolboy I learned about all these things very much from a metropolitan perspective, as it was the linesides of the routes radiating from the capital that gave me my early experience of mainline train watching. What it took me rather longer to realise was that these sections of railway were far from typical, even of the majority of main lines. In fact, I'd started at the very top by becoming familiar with what were not just some of the busiest stretches of trunk railway in Britain but, indeed, in the whole world.

Few model stations needed the services of a dedicated station pilot. Torreyford did!
Author's Collection.

Boat trains are a particular sub-class of main line working, and often went to less-obvious and even remote places. This is the
LNER's 'Flushing Continental' on the way to Harwich; other such destinations included Fishguard in South Wales, Stranraer in Scotland,
Holyhead on Anglesey, Ramsgate in Kent and Fleetwood in Lancashire.
Author's Collection.

It was only when I acquired my first proper bicycle (my father's old Rudge 'Ulster Tourist' - pre-war vintage, blue, with a Chater-Lea chainset, 4-speed Sturmey Archer hub gear and centre-pull brakes) that my horizons widened. There's somehow something about bikes and trains that puts them together in a cosy and natural relationship. Many old railways are now cycle trails, while a surprising number of railway modellers are also keen cyclists. In days of yore, the bicycle was what made train-watching possible, and that old Rudge certainly opened up my horizons. Which was when I found out that not every main line was as exciting a spectacle as the GN on a busy weekday! Not much action and many a lengthy pause was more like it.

Routes that fell into this category were often associated with more rural surroundings. The ex-GE main lines in East Anglia were my 'home territory', but once you got beyond Ipswich, where the Norwich and East Suffolk lines parted, I soon found that the number of trains thinned out more than somewhat. Four or five sightings in an hour was good going, and if you discounted locals or goods trains (ie, anything not hauled by a loco with a tender, Walshaerts valve gear and, preferably, a name) the fare was pretty thin. As my geographi-

cal spread widened still further to incorporate the West Country, Wales and the Southern uplands of Scotland, I soon found that this lack of action was much more the norm. The Waverley route - very much a 'main' line - could be highly spectacular when a train did appear. But that was not very often.

Mainline ambience

Even without a train in sight, though, there always seemed to be a certain 'something' about a main line that distiguished it from lesser routes. One could sense the status of such a railway merely by standing beside it - it had a definite ambience that was unmistakable. Analysing this with the benefit of hindsight, I realise now that - as with many aspects of 'place' - it was the combination of a multitude of factors, some obvious, but many in the form of small and subtle details, that came together to convey this 'feel'.

The first giveaway was the nature of the route itself. A quadruple track was usually a cert, but double track with wide-sweeping canted curves was almost as good a bet. Single tracks, on the other hand, were always dubious. The matter was decided by a myriad of detail. Clues included the state of the track and the lineside - in steam days, usually immaculate. The rails would be bright and shiny from heavy use, the bolts on the fishplates would be gleaming with oil, the ballast was clean and regular and as well-kept as my Grandfather's garden path. (Weeds unkown). Banks and cutting sides were mown and clear of heavy vegetation, fences were in first class order and there were lots of wires on the telegraph pole runs. Other clues included the size and strength of structures like bridges, the types of signals (home over distants were a classic giveaway) and the density of signal wire runs.

Even the modern main line has features that set it apart - although today's clues are perhaps a shade less subtle. Leaving aside the fact that, on a rail network as pared-down as ours the main lines are often all that is left, the physical plant is still distinctive: heavy rail, concrete sleepers, deep ballast and alarming-looking superelevation distinguish the track, with four aspect colour-light signals and AWS magnets and ramps to hint at high-speed intent. The linesides are no longer cared for as they once were, but the rails are as polished as ever even if fishplates are all but unknown. Signalling and telephone cables sneak unseen through concrete troughs, but good fencing is more important than ever in these days of quiet-running trains hitting speeds undreamed-of in steam days.

But what really 'made' the main line was the trains, especially the long-distance passenger trains. The latterday low-season 'Riviera' toiling up through the Cornish woods to Doublebois may only have rated a 'County' or a 'Hall' and passed at a stately 40 m.p.h., but it was still the Cornish Riviera Express. It had nameboards, a restaurant car, matching stock and an air of indefinable importance that hinted at 'Kings' and the dash down Wellington Bank to come. Even a packed holiday special on the East Suffolk line - a B1 or B17 and nine or ten ill-assorted coaches, sometimes of strange (ie., LMS) outline - had that main-line air, for all that it was going no faster or further than the prosaic Ipswich to Lowestoft all-stations. Certainly, if you lingered on that so-convenient loading bank at the down end of Wickham Market station you would be passed mostly by pottering locals, the occasional toiling goods and a few of what the GE loosely termed 'stock' trains (milk, mostly, with parcels and perishables thrown in for good measure) ; but then - joy of joys - would come the banshee shriek of a B17 or - on red-letter days - a Britannia, bearing down at the head of the 'Easterling' at sixty plus. Then one was left in no doubt of the true status of those metals shimmering in the summer sun.

Railway Status

Considering the rank of a railway in terms of its ambience and by the nature of its most important trains opens up a wider spectrum of candidates for possible main line status. The Somerset and Dorset running south from Bath, for instance, for all that it was rural and bucolic - and, in places, only single track - was still very much a 'main line'. How could any line on which trains were sometimes hauled by not one but two Bullied Pacifics be otherwise? By contrast, two other Westcountry routes with which I became well-acquainted were distinguished by division. The SR route from Exeter to Barnstaple was definitely 'main line', for all its twisting route, frequent stations and comparitively slow trains. But the not-dissimilar GW route from Taunton to Barnstaple was never more than a branchline, even on those occasions when it rose to the dizzy heights of a 'named' engine, or if the more usual Mogul essayed an energetic sprint into mile-a-minute realms.

Looking at railways in this way throws up some surprising possibilities for the aspiring main-line modeller - not to mention the odd contrast or contradiction. The GW/LMS joint route from Shrewsbury to Hereford is every inch a main line (and a truly great one to observe if you combined a love of trains with an interest in ornithology), but what of the Central Wales route that left it south of Craven Arms? You couldn't have a more bucolic country station than Knucklas Halt - so what

Milk and perishables were an important main line traffic for many years, especially in the West Country and East Anglia. Here is Pendon's train of 'Siphons' crossing the Brunel timber viaduct on the Dartmoor scene, behind a 'Bulldog' 4-4-0. *Pendon Museum.*

business had a 'Jubilee' to be blasting through on the single line, regulator wide open and Stanier hooter moaning, tailed by a long maroon rake packed with Mancunians headed for the holiday pleasures of the South Wales beaches? And what of the Cambrian route, almost all single track, steeply graded and winding - but boasting the immortal 'Cambrian Coast Express'? The spotless 'Manor' or - in high season - pair of Standard Fours, proudly displaying the headboard at the head of the line of sparkling chocolate-and-cream Mkl coaches (complete with restaurant car), left one in no doubt that this was indeed a 'main line' in the most proper sense.

There are examples a-plenty both of seemingly minor lines that lay claim to the title of 'main' , and important-looking bits of multi-track railway that are actually only of secondary status. The routes up through the South Wales coal valleys, for instance, may have had lots of tracks and lots of trains; but to me they were never 'main' in any sense. No long-distance passenger trains, you see, and never a ten-der loco in sight. No chance. The London suburban lines, intense though the service may have been, were likewise of lesser caste. Hustle and bustle but nowhere much to go didn't make a main line in Rice's book. I suppose at the end of the day my judgements in these matters are very subjective. But for me, to qualify as a main line, a railway had to have those two essentials - the right 'ambience' and at least one regular long-distance passenger train, preferably named. So those are the sort of railways I'm looking at in this book.

Main lines made for modelling

"Fist catch your hare," cautions Mrs Beeton, before describing the method of cooking the unfortunate animal should you succeed. The first step in creating a successful main line model seems to me to be to pick the right sort of subject. And, tempting though the four-track formations of the great trunk lines may be, few of us will ever have the space or resources to attempt them in model form. Usually, the nub of the design exercise is reconciling main-line aspirations with a set of circumstances that are far from ideal for the purpose. Success lies in making the best of a bad job. So - what makes a modellable main line subject?

The over-riding factor has to be: curves. For a start, has your proposed prototype got any? In my book, one of the least suitable of subjects for a model railway is the dead-straight raceway, which is not only near-impossible to replicate in the sort of site most of us have to work with, but also - at least to my eye - lacks visual interest as a model. My experience is that curves are an essential ingredient in successful model railway layouts, main line or otherwise - which unfortunately rules out a few prototypes from the outset, including most of the big trunk lines across open, flat country. I'm not saying such subjects are unmodellable, but they certainly don't sit well on the sort of modest site I'm considering here, which at its most generous gets no larger than a normal domestic garage.

The point is that the essential character of a long, straight section of main line - the NE from York to Northallerton, for instance - is that it is, well - straight. And long. Bung a curve of any sort - let alone a way-too-tight 180° return curve - into the issue, and you've destroyed any hope of producing a convincing representation of that bit of railway. And creating a miniature 'portrait' of the prototype is, for me, the essence of the exercise. I daresay that someone, somewhere has a site a hundred feet long by ten wide (one recalls Richard Chown's layout housed on a disused footbridge at Edinburgh Waverly station), but I'd suggest it's probably rarer than gold-crowned chicken dentures.

A pioneering main line layout using EM gauge in a modest space (approx 15 x 9 feet) was Alfred Bastable's L & Y 'Rawnook'. The L & Y 2-4-2 radial tanks, like that seen here, were built as main line passenger motive power.
Author's Collection.

Trainsets traditionally consist of an express passenger loco and two coaches. No real train was ever made up thus, surely?
Well, here's GWR 6019 'King Henry V' with a 'B' set and a couple of vans behind the tender - being run in after
overhaul on Swindon - Bristol local workings on the GW main line. Truly, anything is possible!
Author's Collection.

Most of us have to contend with layout footprints sitting somewhere in the general range of from 'square or thereabouts' to - if we're lucky - 'well proportioned oblong'. Of which the domestic garage - sixteen by nine feet up to eighteen square - is usually the best that can be hoped for. Most normal attics will liberate a not-dissimilar area to a single garage - maybe a tad wider, but usually little if any longer. To fit any reasonable length of main-line run into such a restricted site is going to require curvature at either end, often severe enough to be of an unseemly nature. Up to a point, such unwanted curves can be hidden, but if you're not careful you'll end up with more track hidden than is visible. A better bet, I've found, is to model something which is curved in reality - there's a big difference between monkeying around with curves that are there in the first place, and sneaking them in where they didn't ought to be.

Of course, one way around this problem is to concoct your own prototype - a tradition with a long and noble history in British railway modelling. Although accurately-researched and dead-to-scale prototype modelling is very much The Thing To Do these days, there are more ways of coming at the 'authenticity' angle than by slavishly copying an actual location. Even something like Pendon is, strictly speaking, 'freelance' - although I fancy few would deign to question its authenticity

or realism. The point is that every element included in Pendon - or any other successful 'fictional but convincing' layout - rings true, including the curvature of the running lines. The trick is to include nothing that the real thing would not have had, and as many as possible of the features typical of that particular prototype. So, given that we will almost certainly need to include curves in our model, it seems logical to seek our inspiration amongst railways characterised in reality by curvature. Like the GWR in the Vale of the White Horse...

Scenic setting

The other factor that makes a section of main line 'modellable' - in both practical and aspirational terms - is the relationship it bears to its surroundings. These days, model railways - of whatever subject or inspiration - are very much about presenting a complete picture; that is, the railway and its setting. This is in contrast to the older tradition where the modelling 'stopped at the boundary fence', and the actual trackage was all that mattered.

There is no doubt that some sorts of scenery are a lot more modellogenic than others. This is a problem clearly exemplified in the USA, where for every model railroad representing the classic midwestern plains (by far the most prevalent landscape type) there are a couple of dozen threading the Rockies

Rice was lucky enough to learn about main lines from the side of some of the busiest trunk routes in the world. Here is rebuilt Royal Scot 'The Honourable Artillery Company' heading an express through Harrow, on the West Coast main route out of Euston; the electrified lines to Watford are in the foreground. *Author's Collection.*

or the Appalachians, or meandering picturesquely through rolling New England or the undulating woodlands of the South. Well, how do you make a visually interesting main line model out of a dead-straight single track running endlessly through a dead flat plain divided up into exact one-mile squares, where the minimal field size is a 'quarter-section' of 160 acres, usually planted with exactly the same crop as all the adjoining 'quarter sections'? Where stations or other 'events' are even more infrequent than the trains, and where the landscape is essentially unchanging for hundreds and hundreds of miles on end? Not easy....

Fortunately, the modeller of the British railway scene has a far wider choice of subject. One of the joys of Britain is the immense variety in landscape even over a relatively short journey, such as the hundred and seventy miles dividing Exeter from London. Going Great Western, your journey starts among the steep-swelling hillsides and red soils of the Culm Valley, toils up through the wooded Blackstone Hills to White Ball Tunnel, then dashes down to Taunton. Cogload junction swings you beneath the Bristol line and launches you through the gentle rises of the Polden Hills, with a wonderful panorama over the Somerset Levels. At Westbury you're on the chalk, with steep short-turved downland at the lineside and prehistoric enigmas carved in the hillsides. The train winds a way through the fringes of Salisbury's eponymous plain, bare-sided cuttings and short tunnels, sweeping embankments and continuous curvature. Then down into the lovely, wide, green valley of the Kennet, with the canal for company lockstepping its way down to the Thames at Reading. Finally, that last thrilling dash through the suburbs to

Brunel's mighty cathedral of a station. By contast, 170 miles on the Midwest Corridor Limited between St Louis and Chicago gets you corn - lots of it.

So even if your chosen prototype is the GW route to Exeter post 1906, then there's a fair variety of possible subject and scenery - including quite a few highly 'modellogenic' locations even for the relatively space-starved. Castle Cary, for instance - junction for the Weymouth line - has been the subject of more than one successful layout, while somewhere like Somerton would make an attractive 'wayside' subject, especially if you could fit that wonderful viaduct in. Westbury, on the other hand, would be a stiff proposition for even the most ambitious, while Hungerford would offer a nice challenge in architectural and canalside modelling.

Main Line ideals

To summarise all these observations into something reasonably pithy is not easy. But, in preparing proposals for this book, my objective has been to select (or dream up) combinations of trackwork, train types, site and scenic setting that are as visually interesting as they are practicable modelling propositions. My aim is to produce schemes that will be capable of providing both an attainable subject for modelling coupled with rewarding operational challenges and - hopefully - an entertaining lineside experience. In undertaking this, I have also set out to make full use of the wonderful range of high-quality models, hi-tech materials, electronic control systems and all the other wonderful ingredients that we are lucky enough to have at our disposal nowadays. Take it from one who started in the days when the only choice was no choice - you never had it so good!

CHAPTER 2

Practicalities

Modest spaces

Having been reasonably precise in defining what I'm considering by way of 'main lines', the first thing that needs sorting out in terms of practicalities is just what sort of a site - in size and proportion - constitutes a 'modest space'. Or, more specifically, how modest a modest space suffices to house a modest main line layout? Rather than pick on arbitrary site sizes for these schemes, I've elected to take a leaf out the pages of the German magazine MIBA (Miniaturbahnen) and to make use of only a series of specific and defined real locations. 'Dreaming up' layout sites always seems to me to be perilously close to cheating, as it's all too easy to make the site fit the layout rather than vice-versa. MIBA presents would-be layout designers with a series of actual rooms, ranging from the 'Keller' (cellar) to the 'Kinderzimmer' (children's bedroom,

a space of statutory size and form in German homes and hence a commonly-available site). All 'theoretical' MIBA layout proposals have to fit one or other of these locations - including allowing due access to doorways, windows, closets and so on.

For a book such as this to be relevant - and hence of any conceivable use - it is necessary to keep one's feet firmly on terra firma when it comes to not just the dimensions of the prospective layout site, but also its nature. Modern model railways have to function in a social as well as a practical sense, and a certain amount of compromise is often needed to reconcile the needs of other family members with the spatial demands of the layout. Not to mention steering clear of problems with the neighbours or the local building control officer, or doing anything that would devalue the house or make it

A sharp-ish curve on the prototype (although not that tight - there's no check-rail) with a local passenger train hauled by an LMS 'Crab' 2-6-0 coming under the bridge. This is a very common situation on many model railways, and the picture gives a useful indication as to what looks right. I'd estimate that in 00 gauge, a three-foot curve would give the right effect.
F Ashley/Author's Collection.

unsaleable. Which rules out several of the expedients suggested from time to time in the olden-day model railway press, like bashing holes through walls, carrying out DIY and structurally questionable attic conversions, running tracks along hallways and across landings, or doing without basic domestic facilities to make room for the railway! Well, who needs a bathroom anyway?

Sites for a main line layout

So for this book I've worked around what I hope are some typical but attainable sites. The first is one I'm often faced with designing for - the third bedroom of a typical British 3-bedroom 'semi', probably our nearest equivalent to the German 'Kinderzimmer'. In many houses built from the 1930s onwards, this third bedroom (usually situated above the entrance hall) was very small indeed - from as little as six feet square upwards. Six by eight feet with a window in one short wall and the door in a corner of the wall opposite seems to be a fairly typical, so I've taken this as my minimalist starting point (N gauge modellers only need apply!). Seven by ten feet (or two by three metres, if you're really with it) is a slightly more generous version of the same thing - quite a common size in a lot of modern homes, and just about the bottom limit for 00 in this context. Last entry in the bedroom site stakes is the larger size normally found in the same type of house - typically of the order of fourteen by ten feet, sometimes with the bonus of a bay window.

Moving downstairs usually offers few possibilities for the aspiring main line modeller, but step outside into the garden and things look up considerably. Cyril Freezer was always a great champion of the common-or-garden shed as a viable layout site, and I find that at least in this I'm at one with him. They are available in a huge range of sizes, formats and qualities, are relatively cheap to buy and not usually a problem to accommodate even in a small garden. Sheds are readily adapted to modelling purposes, easily insulated, and don't usually need any form of planning permission - provided they aren't on a 'permanent foundation'. Ten by six feet is about the smallest practicable size for any sort of main line layout, but the next size up - twelve by eight feet - is really quite a useful and manageable space. A further advantage of the garden shed is that it reduces the impact of the model on other members of the household and usually passes unnoticed and unremarked by the rest of the world. And yes, I do my own modelling in a shed!

The next logical step up in site is a rather bigger sort of shed or - put another way - a garage. Sixteen by nine feet was the standard size for an older single-car garage, with more recent examples a bit more generous at around 7.5 x 3m (roughly 18ft 6ins x 10 foot). I've used the smaller site, but with the proviso that all the 'garage' proposals have a 'squeeze allowance' to enable them to be eased out a bit for the larger size. If you're very lucky, you might gain uncontested possession of a double garage, which gives a site around 18 feet square.

Apart from their sheer size, garages form a very useful sort of site with a number of advantages - not the least of which is two nice big doors to move the layout, people and materials in and out of the building when required. Usually, they have a solid, reasonably level floor and often power ready laid on. Even if separate and free-standing, they're not too difficult to insulate and heat (there are some very effective and efficient new halogen space heaters made for this purpose these days - a lot of car-restoration enthusiasts use them.) Garages that are attached to or integrated with a house are even better, as they are relatively easy to incorporate into the normal domestic central heating system. Luxury! The chief disadvantage in using the garage is that you have to leave the car outside - although with modern cars this is not really a problem. In fact, even with older cars (such as those driven by the likes of Rice, usually well into their third decade), it's no bad thing. It's often said that the worse thing

you can do to any car is put it away wet in a sealed garage. Well, that's my excuse, anyway...

Otherwise, the largest site usually encountered in normal homes is the attic, where this lends itself to adaptation. Which, increasingly in these days of lightweight gang-nailed roof trusses, it doesn't - unfortunately. But older houses with traditional rafters and purlins can offer real scope, and even quite a modest dwelling can offer a decent size of site in the roof. I've taken my friend John Chambers' 17 x 11 foot loft as a good median size, although in this case the roof is a conventional pitched one rather than the common hipped type, which doesn't offer quite the scope or ease of adaptation. Arranging an adequately strong floor, sufficient ventilation for comfort and a good standard of insulation are the main problems with an attic; modern folding or slide-away access ladders make it relatively easy to get up and down.

So - these are the various 'example' sites for which I've penned these designs, aiming to come up with the best all-round combination of subject, scale and size in each case. Generally speaking, it's the smallest dimension of the site which is the limiting factor, as it's that which determines the possible radii of the all-important curves. The length can usually be 'fiddled' a bit, but if there isn't enough room for the necessary curve radii then it's creek and paddle time, I'm afraid.

Curves, curves, dam' curves

Track curvature is, by and large, the bane of our modelling lives. Even the most parsimonious of prototype engineers opted for curve radii that were more than generous when considered in model railway terms. Indeed, in a classic textbook on the topic of railway civil engineering ('Railway Construction', by W Hemingway Mills, Longman's Civil Engineering Series, published in1898), the 'normal' curve suggested on a main running line of railway 'in open country' is 60 chains - a jot over 50 ft radius in 4mm! Mills also notes that, in preparing plans for deposition before Parliament, it was a requirement to 'mark the exact radius of any curve below one mile (80 chains) in radius'. Food for thought... Of course, in difficult country, such generous curves were not always possible, but never-

Very linear things are trains - especially on straight track. This lengthy express (possibly a Newmarket race 'special') on the ex-GE Cambridge line near Whitlesford is double-headed by 'Sandringham' 2819 'Welbeck Abbey' and unrebuilt 'Claud' 8797. Thirteen coaches are visible. *Real Photographs/Ian Allan.*

theless main lines rarely got below about 12 chains radius - something over ten foot in 4mm scale.

Fortunately for us, however, this is one aspect of the prototype that we do not need to translate literally in a model. Indeed, if we did represent our curves exactly to scale they would not look right, as perceived curvature is one of those things greatly affected by perspective and viewpoint. And as a model represents the prototype as seen from a moderately distant viewpoint (how distant depending upon scale and viewing distance), then we need to curve our model tracks to give the right effect rather than to be mathematically exact. This manipulation is something that is very difficult to measure other than by eye - so I offer no magic formulae for arriving at values which will 'look right'. But what I will say is that - fortunately - we can get away with an amazing degree of compression and exaggeration before things start to jar too much, especially in 00 and N gauges.

Curve constraints

So, what are the visual give-aways that scream 'Too tight!" when a model train enters or rounds a curve? I would pick lateral displacement as the chief culprit, something which manifests itself in several ways - all painfully obvious. The first is lateral acceleration, when the train 'whips' into a curve by way of a violent deflection that would do rather more than spill the soup in the restaurant car; put everyone out of their seats onto the floor with their luggage flying everywhere is more like it! Secondly, the visibility of the coach ends and their relative movement one to another is an all-too-obvious and related

anomaly, while the relationship of the mid-point of the coaches to the track can also look decidedly uncomfortable if the curve radius is inadequate.

Look at your train and ask yourself: are you aware of the coach-ends as the train enters the curve or comes toward you around it? This is something that virtually never happens in reality, and is made worse by greater-than-scale (and often greater-than-necessary) coupling distances and by the common situation where the coach ends are a different colour to the sides. Secondly, is the radius such that the outside rail is visible and exposed below the centre of the coach when it's on the curve? That's another situation that simply does not occur on prototype running lines. In pure practical terms, such excessive displacements can manifest themselves even more forcibly - when your coaches clout each other end-to-midpoint when passing on double-tracked curves!

In fact, I'd argue that the limit on the visible curvature one can reasonably use on a main line layout is dictated far more by considerations of appearance than by the tightness of whatever outlandish corner you can actually persuade your trains to squeak around. There are any number of tricks and devices that can be used to reduce the practical impact of over-tight curves - excessive coupling gaps or clever 'get bigger round the bend' type couplers, offset bogie pivots, less-than-scale length vehicles (the train set favourite) and overscale track centres. But however well they work in practice, these dodges always look awful. Conversely, a curve that looks reasonable will almost always be practicable; this is another of those aspects of railway modelling - fortunately widespread -

Modern RTR coaches are - unlike their
predecessors - of scale dimensions.
Here is a Bachmann 'Bulleid', a scale
61ft 6ins long; ten inches
of layout length.
Author.

where the old maxim 'if it looks OK it'll work OK' holds good.

But there are curves and curves, and sometimes the obvious answer is not the best one. Take a fairly typical 'modest main line layout' situation, where it is necessary to squeeze a double-tracked 180° return curve into a maximum site width of around 8ft in 4mm scale. Given that you can't realistically (or often prudently) take the trackage to the extreme edge of the layout, a reasonable compromise would be to use 7ft 6ins or so of this width to contain the trackage. Fine, you could argue, no problem; radius of outer track a tad under 3ft 9ins, with the inner one somewhere around the 3ft 7in mark. Not that tight... Except that a train travelling in a straight line at a reasonable-looking scale speed (more on that thorny topic in a page or two...) will deviate with neck-snapping suddenness if led straight onto a circular curve of this radius at that same speed. Oh, it won't derail or anything drastic, but it certainly won't look convincing.

On the face of it there are two possible answers to this common conundrum: slow the train down or ease the curve. Option one is easy enough - except that the speed which looks 'right' for the curve will almost certainly lack sufficient 'hustle' down the straight, undermining the illusion we're trying to convey. Given that real trains accelerate and decelerate over a span of minutes and miles rather than seconds and feet, adjusting the speed as the train enters the curve won't help the realism quotient much, either. So - can the curve itself be eased? Not without a wider site. But what if rather than trying to ease the whole curve one simply concentrates on easing the entry, aiming to avoid any sudden change of direction?

Transitions - the desirable deviation

This is what the real thing does; bends are entered by a transition - a parabolic form of curve with a gradually tightening radius. Realigning our curve from a simple semi-circle of fixed radius to a semi-ellipse may result in a smaller 'limiting radius' at the tightest part of the curve - but will also avoid an unseemly and unrealistic deflection in the path of the train as it runs onto the curve. Provided that the train will still physically negotiate the 'limiting radius', the practicalities aren't affected, but the visual impression (aka 'realism') is greatly enhanced. And if the train looks a tad uncomfortable at the apex of the resulting bend, then this is the section of track to hide; on the oval-based layout format most often suited to mainline subjects, this 'squeeze' at the extreme apexes is far easier to disguise than an abrupt lurch as the train enters the curve - something that usually happens 'stage front' and very visibly.

Adjusting curves so that the entries are eased is a well worthwhile in a main line context. Indeed, I'd argue that it's usually essential. Another useful ploy in maintaining the main line illusion is to avoid any transitions from dead-straight to what will inevitably be sharply-curved track. I'm not saying this is totally unprototypical - but it's certainly not a common characteristic of the majority of railways. The reason is obvious - the speed which can be run on dead straight metals is far higher than that which is tolerable on curves, especially tight ones. So the best and most efficient solution in real railway terms - where unnecessary acceleration and deceleration are a waste of time and

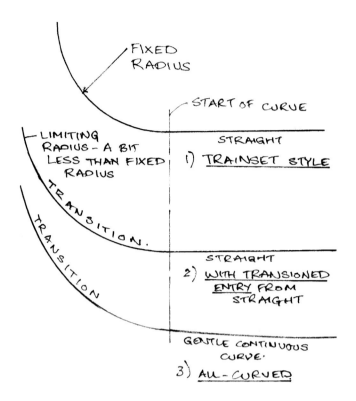

FIXED RADIUS

START OF CURVE

LIMITING RADIUS - A BIT LESS THAN FIXED RADIUS

STRAIGHT
1) TRAINSET STYLE

TRANSITION.

TRANSITION

STRAIGHT
2) WITH TRANSIONED ENTRY FROM STRAIGHT

GENTLE CONTINUOUS CURVE.
3) ALL-CURVED

fuel - is to lay out a route suited to a particular median steady speed rather than one calling for constant adjustment toward either extreme.

This type of continuous but easy curvature is something that often marks out more mature railways. When Stephenson, Locke & Co were surveying their first lines in the1830s and 40s, the maximum speed of the steam locomotive was something less than 40 m.p.h. You couldn't go any faster than that however straight the track, therefore so as long as the curves were compatible with this limited terminal velocity, you were OK. Hence the 'straight linked by kink' alignments they often plotted for these pioneer railways. The exception was, of course, Brunel - who was thinking in terms of 60+ m.p.h. on his super-stable broad gauge from the outset, with more to come as things developed. Which is why modern HSTs can run at 125 m.p.h. over Brunel's original alignments, even on the 'narrow gauge' .....

Apart from all other considerations, the sort of sinuous alignment that characterises many railways in typical undulating British terrain is visually attractive, and gives a pleasing sense of movement to the trains. The fact that such alignments are often associated with (relatively) lower speeds - as on the GW main line through Cornwall, for instance, or over routes like the immortal Settle and Carlisle - is a bonus for us in the context of our modest main line layouts. If you only have a limited field of view available, do you really want your trains to belt through it in a few tenths of a second? To my eye, a smooth, but steady progress through the scene is both more rewarding and more realistic.

Length - or the lack thereof

The other bugbear of railway modelling in general, but main-line modelling in particular, is the knotty problem of train length. While a two-coach branchline train pulled by a small tank engine causes few layout design problems, it's a very different proposition when you need to accommodate a twelve-coach express pulled by a pacific. Two pacifics, if it's the S & D! It's not just the train length that's the problem, it's the relationship that this bears to all the other aspects of the layout design. Long trains and small sites make unhappy bedfellows, as it's not just the visual imbalance that grates but such hard practical considerations as fiddleyard storage, platform lengths, clearance points and the limits placed on gradients and curves.

The problem with real railways is that they are essentially very linear things. Their footprint is effectively infinitely long by exceedingly thin. Model railways, as already remarked, are very often quite otherwise. Like your author, they have proportions that can be summarised as 'too short, too wide'. This is an intractable incompatibility that has dogged the development of model railways since the days of Bing. And it is something that has become more and more of a problem as standards of authenticity among all classes of models have risen. The sort of distortions that characterised 'toy' trains (and differentiated them clearly from 'scale models') were almost always in the matter of length.

Early commercial products such as Bing and Hornby were usually little more than charming caricatures, ridiculously short in relation to their width and height. Hornby Dublo was considerably better; the locos were at least dimensionally accurate, even if the coaches were somewhat truncated. Trix, on the other hand, almost never got their proportions right, while most Triang models started out as runts. Even as late as the early 1980s, a substantial proportion of the rolling stock offered in RTR form (not to mention more than a few kits!) was of less than scale length. Only with the arrival of 'new generation' RTR from the mid-1980s onwards could you buy a coach that was correct in this fundamental - the honours going, I fancy, to Airfix, with the GW 'Centenary' stock, the 'B set' and the auto-trailer. Nowadays, of course, we're spoilt for choice; the accuracy and quality of something like a Bachmann BR Mk 1 or a Hornby Pullman car is above reproach.

Which means that the problem just got worse. Or rather, one of the traditional 'solutions' - short stock - has to be discounted. There is now no readily-discernible difference in fidelity between RTR, kit and handbuilt stock in this important area. Often, given our need for a greater coupling distance to accommodate our too-tight curves, our models end up being actually longer than the strict scale equivalent of the real thing! Not helpful. With train lengths being thus immutable, we can only foreshorten them by using less than the 'correct' number of vehicles. Or by choosing subjects or situations where shorter trains are authentic. That's my preferred option, on which more in the next chapter.

CHAPTER 3

Pragmatism

Having kicked around the possibilities and practicalities of the main-line themed layout for a few pages, it's now time to start to draw some conclusions as to what, realistically, can be attempted in our modest domestic site. Time, in other words, to face up to reality and choose which of a range of unwelcome compromises you are prepared to accept. For compromises there will have to be if anything is to be achieved in the context of a main line in a modest space - compromises in scale fidelity, standards, scope and operational potential. So, to try and identify the potential of this sort of layout, it seems a reasonable idea to take a pragmatic look at what you might term the 'median situation' - a typical set of ingredients for such a model railway.

Scale, Gauge and Standards

This 'median' is something which will vary from scale to scale, so that's the first thing to consider. In the context of this book, I'm really thinking around 00 and N, although some of the 4mm proposals could at a pinch be executed in EM or even P4, while most of the N scale designs would work equally well in 2mm finescale. 3mm scale - neglected by the mainstream but very much alive and kicking - would slot neatly between the two. In fact, any of these 00 designs, executed in 3mm finescale (13.5 or 14.2mm gauge, the 3mm equivalents to EM or P4) would give the best of all worlds in terms of realism, spaciousness and maximum fidelity on a given site. The snag with 3mm is, of course, that there's not much in the way of RTR to give you a leg-up, although a surprisingly wide range of kits is available.

What you can get away with in terms of workable main line layout design criteria ultimately comes down to the particular recipe you elect to cook your model to. If it must be in high-end 4mm scale to P4 standards, featuring 70ft stock with full working corridor connections and hauled by fully detailed 'Kings' or other seriously large locomotives, then there is no way that you'll be able to negtiate the two foot six inch radius

Main lines are not just about express passenger trains - there are all manner of other workings to represent, like this express goods on the ex-GE main line at Brentford Bank. The locomotive is a class B12 4-6-0, a definite 'passenger engine'; such types were often used for freight working, but trains such as this are rarely modelled. *Author's Collection.*

Main lines were host to all manner of lesser workings; here's a pick-up freight at Norton Fitzwarren, on the main line from Bristol to Exeter.
Author's Collection.

curve that is the ultimate practicable bottom limit for main line 00. Double that figure (at least!) is more like it. Similarly - given that you will naturally be replicating prototype train formations exactly with scale-length stock - is there any scope for pruning the length needed. So a layout based on such a precept will inevitably be space-hungry - not to mention time consuming and costly. For that reason, such an essay is rarely practicable for modellers contending with normal domestic settings, the usual chronic lack of spare time and a modest budget.

O gauge also misses out in this context. The phrases 'main line', '7mm scale' and 'modest spaces' don't sit well in the same sentence. To create a convincing O gauge main line layout demands even more by way of site than the direct ratio of size and scale would suggest. Six feet is often quoted as the practicable mimimum curvature, but to convicingly represent a main line curve at least ten feet or thereabouts is really needed. Not to mention sufficient length to accommodate twenty feet or more of train! Which is why main line layouts in O gauge tend to be built by clubs or those fortunate few individuals who can afford them. They are also often partly or wholly located outside in the garden - where space is not such a concern

and scenic modelling is done with a spade. Either way, I'm afraid they lie outside the scope of this book.

The apt choice of scale and standards is an immutable one. No amount of wishful thinking or clever dodging will buck a fundamental incompatibility of subject, scale and site. This is a point on which I frequently find myself taking issue with those who blithely assert that 'building a layout in P4 is no more difficult than in 00' or that '00 (or N) is fundamentally innacurate and should be banned' or - dafter still - that '00 should be 19mm gauge' (which would not only wipe out all its considerable advantages but introduce a whole raft of new compromises and difficulties). In fact, the reason why there are relatively few fine scale main line layouts (in any size) is precisely because it is so much more demanding to work to these standards. Conversely, the fact that 00 and N permit you to take certain highly-relevant liberties commend them greatly in this application.

4mm scale candidates
So, to start in middle-of-the-road 4mm scale, the sort of subjects I'd suggest are practicable within a domestic environment centre mostly around what might be termed 'lesser' main

lines - that is, routes that carry express long-distance passenger trains, but are not of the first importance as trunk arteries. Nevertheless, these are railways of definite main line status, characterised by their infrastructure and the nature of their train service. In remoter areas, such as those served by the Highland or Cambrian railways, the actual railway may only have been heavily-graded single track offering considerable operating challenges. But a quick glance at the map (plus their continued existence today when far grander routes have gone) shows their importance. Fortunately for we modellers, such 'lesser' main lines formed a very substantial portion of Britain's railway network, and consequently offer a huge range of possibilities.

Examples of the sort of subject I'm trying to categorise would include the GWR main line in Cornwall, or the same company's routes from Yeovil to Weymouth or from Gloucester to Hereford. The ex-GE East Suffolk line would qualify, as would such 'joint' classics as the M & GN or Somerset and Dorset. The ex-GC main line to London was never more than lesser, I fear, while the Southern's wandering limb stretching into Cornwall and North Devon became aptly known as the 'Withered Arm'. Further north, one can cite an enticing string of such prototypes: almost anything in Scotland north of the Edinburgh - Glasgow corridor and several lines - such as the Waverly Route and the G & SW 'Port Road' - south of it. The NER route across the Pennines to Carlisle fits the bill, as do lots of bits of the L & Y and the entire Furness Railway route from Lancaster to Carlisle via Barrow. The Midland has some classic candidates, from the brave Settle and Carlisle to that spectacular traverse of the Peak District between Derby and Manchester. Wales offers the Cambrian, the Fishguard line and the Shrewsbury and Hereford up through the borders.

Even in the South-East, the tangle of relatively short routes from London to the Kent and Sussex coastlines harbour a surprising array of candidates.

To put things in a more practical context, for 4mm scale I'm looking at railways where the nature of the route gives a curving single or double-track formation, running through an interesting and modellogenic setting. I'm looking for enough variety and density of traffic to offer rewarding operation without calling for a vast stocklist or a monster fiddleyard to handle the 'offstage' workings. The principal main line trains need to be of a relatively modest order, no more than around eight coaches, with correspondingly limited formations for secondary and non-passenger workings. I'm also looking for subjects that offer a good balance between the various aspects of the layout, both visually and in terms of the work and expenditure needed. And where I haven't been able to find an actual location that fits this list of requirements, I've gone my usual heretical way and made something up.

2mm Scale

The chief joy of 2mm scale in a main line context is that even big prototypical train formations come out a manageable length when related to typical domestic sites. This makes possible the truly compact main-line layout without the need to compromise on train formations, platform lengths, curve radii and so on. On larger domestic sites - such as the 'garage' or 'attic' - the possibilities in N are far-reaching and embrace railways right up to trunk line status. So the choice of prototype is, at that end of the scale, correspondingly wider. So is the possibility of sticking with a lesser prototype but modelling a lot more of it in a typically Transatlantic approach. I've explored both these options in my proposals.

Like Pullmans? These were quite often seen on lesser main lines - notably as 'specials' to race meetings or premier holiday trains. On the GE lines, Pullman race specials went to Newmarket, while the 'Eastern Belle' served the premier North Norfolk Coast resorts.
Author's Collection.

Where the smaller scale offers less scope is in the representation of more offbeat prototypes. The 4mm modeller has not only a wonderful selection of very good quality RTR models to choose from, he also has a huge range of kits available to him. These days, it's almost quicker to list prototypes for which you can't get a 4mm kit than to try and cover the possibilities. The choice available in 2mm scale is only a fraction of this, and many of these are older, cruder kits that don't quite hack it in today's sophisticated market. However, N is still relatively well off in terms of RTR models, and at the present time we are seeing great advances in the quality and variety of these. At last, a couple of real bugbears of the standard are being addressed, with a much finer wheel profile appearing on recent introductions. The standard of finish and detail is also improving, which only leaves the matter of a far less obtrusive and far more versatile coupling to be addressed.

2mm scale has also always attracted a small but dedicated band of modellers whose craftsmanship never fails to astound. In terms of main line modelling, several of the very finest examples have been in 2mm fine scale, notably 'Chiltern Green' and 'Copenhagen Fields' from the Model Railway Club in London and the breathtaking 'Chee Tor' (based on that Derby-Manchester route and hence just the sort of theme I'm championing here) from Manchester. However, one has to acknowledge that tackling the earlier grouping steam era and - more particularly - the pre-group period in 2mm scale is a challenge relatively few can meet. When it comes to the more contemporary scene, however, the reverse is true, and in many ways diesel locomotives, together with large modern rolling stock, long trains and fixed-formation trainsets like HSTs, form a very natural subject for the small scale. Those are possibilities I've sought to exploit in some of these proposals; these days, I even try my own hand at modern-era modelling in N from time to time. I am qualified to join the HST owners club...

Cutting the Cloth

When wangling many a main line into a modest site one sometimes needs a flexible approach to the train length conundrum. Fortunately, it is possible to fiddle things a little bit as the formation of many trains varied from day to day in accord with the actual traffic offering. For instance, something as simple as changing the season of the year represented on the model might be enough to circumvent a difficult. A popular holiday express that loaded to fifteen or more coaches in high summer might well be truncated to a third this length out of season. The Cornish Riviera and Cambrian Coast Express already mentioned were good examples of this. I've already mentioned the 'Riviera', which - either side of the summer - was rarely more than 8 coaches and a 'Hall' once it got west of Plymouth, while the spring 'Cambrian Coast Express' shrank from 11 or so to 5 coaches and a GW small prairie (although still resplendent with headboard, naturally!)

Another obvious ploy is to vary the actual location modelled to accord with the train length you can accommodate. Set out to represent the immortal 'Atlantic Coast Express' in the full summer formation twixt Salisbury and Exeter and you're looking at a 16-coach monster behind a pounding Merchant Navy. Model the Padstow portion of the same train jogging on from Halwill Junction and six coaches would be the limit, with a Light Pacific or maybe only a modest mogul at the head; take that slightly out of season and the six coaches would be three, and the train engine a veteran T9 or a new BR Standard '4' 2-6-4T. It would be a pretty small main line layout that couldn't cope with that!

The ultimate 'glamour' working has to be the Royal Train, and that could go just about anywhere on state or private duties. Here is the LNWR train in transit between Wolferton (for Sandringham) and Balmoral, at the start of what must have been one of its longer trips. The engines are the two 'Super Claud' 4-4-0s, 8783 and 8787, kept by the LNER at Cambridge shed especially for the Royal Train or other special duties.
Author's Collection.

Trunk working on as trunk line; an up LNER East Coast express behind a Gresley A3.
loaded to 12/13 coaches pus a van. A big train in any scale.

Going back in time is another useful option as pre-grouping express trains are a very compact breed. In the first decade of the twentieth century, coaches rarely exceeded 50 feet in length and typically ran in short rakes of five or so vehicles. Lines like the Midland or Great Central ran frequent services of such short trains, hauled by correspondingly modest loco-motives. At 4mm scale, such a flyweight express would scale out at a modest five feet or less. Even many a 'crack' train long-distance train was limited to no more eight or ten such vehicles, behind a 4-4-2 or 4-6-0 of modest dimensions. Things did get a bit more long-winded when longer coaches - up to 70ft on the GWR - came in; but then, there were usually less of them. Only on lines like the LNWR (where they reckoned 40 m.p.h. was quite fast enough for any express, thank you) did they go in for seriously long trains. The Irish Mail of the 1890s seemed frequently to consist of twenty or so ill-assort-ed four, six and eight-wheel coaches and vans, toiling along behind a perspiring Webb Compound and piloted, doubtless, by a stout 'Jumbo'.

Believable train formations

Most of us, in setting out to model the main line in the first place, are merely anxious to be able to run trains that are typical and believable and represent our favourite subjects. I suspect that most of us will also be old nostalgics like me, and will hence have a yen for a proper rake of the sort of carriages we can remember - the later grouping types or, typically, the splendid BR Mk1s - behind a reasonably impressive piece of motive power, whether that's a 'Royal Scot', a Britannia or a Class 50. So just what sort of a train can we assemble using these sort of ingredients, and how is it best made up?

For any scheduled main line working there was usually a 'core' rake of vehicles that had to be there to accommodate the basic classes of traffic carried or to provide essential facilities - catering, luggage capacity, toilets, etc. This core formation was then strengthened as required by additional 'ordinary carriages' to provide sufficient seating for the numbers and classes of passenger offering on a particular day. One of the joys of the traditional loco-hauled passenger train was it was

Big train in pre-group days; an LNWR Webb compound on Bushey troughs with the 'Irish Mail', which could load to 20+ assorted 6-wheel and bogie vehicles.
F.Moore postcard/Author's Collection.

possible to vary trains in this way to match the needs of traffic, often at very short notice - a facility now but a fading memory in these days of universal fixed-formation (and as a result frequently overcrowded) trainsets.

The core vehicles on any traditional express service would include one or more 'brake' vehicles with luggage space and accommodation for the guard, one or more vehicles offering first class accommodation for 'premium travellers'; rather more ordinary second class seating (although the ratio of first to second class seating was widely variable, depending on the nature of the service) and restaurant or buffet car facilities. Thus, even at its most pared-down, a main line express train of the post group/BR era was unlikely to drop below about five coaches. So, at basics, a plausible 'minimal express' would go something along the lines of: Brake composite, all-first or composite, restaurant or buffet car, second, brake second. An example of just such a formation would be the out-of-season Cambrian Coast Express already mentioned.

Normally, there would be rather more ordinary accommodation offered and studying photos and videos of express workings in the1950s suggests an eight-coach formation was pretty typical; the summer-only 'Easterling' already mentioned (Liverpool Street to Yarmouth, with a Lowestoft portion detached at Beccles) was usually made up thus - in my day, eight carmine-and-cream Gresley coaches behind a 'Sandringham' or 'B1'. What more could one ask? Such an eight-coach train usually went something along the lines of: Brake composite, all-first, composite, restaurant car, composite, second, second, brake second. Stick a 4-6-0 on the front and you've got an everyday British main line train of the period 1925 - 1965. Principal services on trunk main lines would be longer, of course, typically loading to ten or twelve coaches behind a 4-6-2, but it was only at peak times - summer holiday 'high season', Christmas and so on - that the real monster trains of fifteen coaches or more were usually seen.

The average British main line coach of the period was between 57 and 70 feet long. Taking sixty-three feet as a rule of thumb gives you 254mm per coach in 4mm scale - ten inches. The same ten inches also covers most express loco-motives including all 4-6-0s except 'Kings' and 'Nelsons'; if you allow eleven inches for your locomotive you'll accom-modate anything this side of a Stanier pacific, which - at 73-

feet (11.5ins) odd over buffers - was the longest British express type. I've always used this ten-inch per coach/loco figure as my estimating value in calculating train lengths, thus far without problem. In 4mm scale, the 'typical' express of 8 coaches plus engine thus comes out at 90ins or seven foot six. Co-incidentally, for modellers of the current scene, a normal 7-car HST formation is almost exactly the same length. This seven and a half foot train length is not too unmanageable even on a modest site, and consequently is the value around which I've worked most of the 4mm schemes in this book. In N scale, of course, the same train formations are a mere 3ft 9ins or so - especially if you take the trouble to close up the grossly overscale coupling gap between coaches.

Stations? Who needs 'em?

For many years, the majority of model railways have been centred around the representation of a station. Several stations, in the spacious days of Beal & Co. Main line layouts have also tended followed this trend, with varying degrees of success. However, in these days of less layout space combined with greater authenticity, scale-length stock, correct train formations and so on it is getting more and more difficult to reconcile the desire to model a station with the space needed to do so convincingly. Given that principal stations normally boasted platform faces long enough to take the longest normal service train with room to spare, the site needed is often far from modest. The main platforms at Torreyford station on the old North Devonshire, for instance, were nearly 14 feet long - longer than a lot of these layouts in total. And even then the 'Torreyman' was still a tight fit when fully laden (16 coaches behind a King).

Of course, not every wayside station on a main line was able to take the full formation of the principal trains using that line. The major trains would not normally be stopping at such places, so the accommodation offered only had to suffice for local workings over the route. David Jenkinson's EM 'Garsdale Road' layout (based on Dent) was a good example of a main line design centred on a smaller station - probably the most realistic option where space is limited and a station is deemed essential. Another approach - which I first suggested in my original layout design book over a decade ago - is not to try and model the whole station, but merely to show the platform ends - which was where the action was, in trainspotting terms. Or you could model part of the approach trackwork - with sidings, signals, complex pointwork, interesting structures and so on - but no actual platforms. Suggesting something without necessarily modelling it is always a useful ploy. But I have found that it's quite possible to make an interesting and very operable main line layout without needing to represent a space-consuming station at all.

So - if you're not going to model a station, what else is there by way of subject? Well, I have seen main line layouts consisting of little more than a suitable section of track passing through some nicely-modelled lineside scenery, which is fair enough if you want to re-live the 'trainspotting experience'. Although, that said, as I recall it we always used to aim to watch from locations where other entertainments were on offer to fill in the time between watch-worthy trains. A favourite was a lie-bye siding or loop, where a freight might be held to allow faster traffic to pass. With luck, you could chat to the driver and maybe get

Flyweight mainline express on the Great Central's London Extension - a handsome 4-4-0 and 5-6 fifty-foot coaches. Less than six feet in total at 4mm scale.
F Moore postcard/Author's Collection.

to stand briefly upon the footplate. Level crossings were another useful standby, when there was road traffic to observe as well as rail, and the closing of the gates gave due notice of the arrival of a train. Lineside industries - especially rail-connected ones - offered further visual variety and perhaps a works shunter, such as the fascinating fireless engine that toiled beside the GE Cambridge lines at - I think - Ponder's End.

But probably top of my list of 'non station' themes for model railways is a junction, which introduces a second route into the equation as well as offering interesting visual possibilities including worthwhile signalling and maybe some challenging trackwork. Combine a junction with a lye-bye, a level crossing and some industrial sidings, and you have an ideal trainwatching location. What better subject for a platform-free mainline model railway? Only a main line junction beside a locomotive depot, I suspect.

Train speeds
Trains going fast have always been a lot of the attraction of watching from the side of a main line; the chance of serious speed was the thing that drew youthful connoisseurs of steam such as Rice to the GN's racetrack, for all that it took twenty-five long miles of pedalling. But it was worth the perspiration for the sight of an A4 at the head of a southbound express bearing down on Hadley Wood or Welwyn at 80 plus, with the three-cylinder rhythm a swift syncopated purr and the exhaust steam streaming out over the carriage roofs - as stirring a sight as one could wish for, even if the experience was all

over, done and dusted in under a minute. (I'll pass up on the obvious allusions here...)

In later years, when the Gresley pacific had given way to a Deltic (easily the most charismatic of main line diesels, in my book) the passing of such a train remained a memorable sensation; who could fail to be impressed by 3,300hp and all those cylinders? Even a common-or-garden HST has that express 'feel', especially when those Paxman Valentas are working hard. The same is not, alas, true of more recent arrivals; being passed by a 'Voyager' - no matter how fast it might be voyaging - has all the aural and visual impact of a string of vacuum cleaners going by.

You may well ask why I'm raising the issue of operating speeds at all in an essay relating to layout design. Well, I'd suggest that speed is a factor which has a fundamental bearing on the nature of a proposed layout. It's not just a case of making sure that what is being designed will physically allow of the desired speeds, but also of whether the result will look natural and convincing or dam' silly and toy-like. Leaving aside such factors as steadiness of running, secure trackholding, lack of wobble or 'shimmy' - all classic model railway failings - what are we looking to achieve on the speed front? In a word - illusion; the 'feel' of a train bearing down and roaring by, so far as is possible in something lacking sound, mass, inertia and the slipstream to set the lineside grasses rippling and rubbish beside the PW flying.

Trying to replicate the feel and impulsion of a real main line express passing at speed in miniature is not the easiest shot to call. For a start, how fast is fast? The question of 'scale

Archetypal pre-group express - GE again, I'm afraid - but a wonderful mix of stock including luggage container wagons and a luggage van - so probably a boat train.
F Moore postcard/Author's Collection.

The 'Lakes Express' of the Furness Railway - not far, not fast, but very much a premier train. The formation here is nine six-wheelers behind a Sharp Stewart 4-4-0.
F Moore postcard/Author's Collection.

speed' has been hotly debated for years in model railway circles. Does one merely scale the distance, or should the time factor also be altered? What is a 'scale' equivalent of 60 m.p.h., for example? Given that this equates to the famous mile a minute (which was usually taken as the threshold of express speeds) then logic would suggest that if our model train traversed a scale mile in a minute the ratio would be right. Well, in 4mm scale, a mile equates to a shade under 70 ft. So our train would need to be travelling at an actual speed of 70ft/min or1.16 feet per second - which is about 0.79 m.p.h. Not very exciting, and unlikely to be suggestive of high speed whatever the scale!

There is another line of argument that runs that the speed of an object is absolute and unrelated to its size, so a model train travelling at a 'scale' sixty will therefore be going at exactly the same speed as the real thing, ergo 88 ft/second. Which means, on many of the layouts proposed here, that it will pass through the field of view in something under two-tenths of a second. Wow! Is your tracklaying that good? Or your eyesight? I think

that's another one that can be discounted... Which leaves the 'double scaled factor' approach, which all my mathematical/scientific mates tell me is a load of tosh, as you cannot meaningfully scale time. Well, what do you scale it by? The size ratio? That's one factor often advanced, which would make a '4mm scale minute' about 0.8 seconds and mean that our 60 m.p.h. 'bogey speed' would need to be one that covered our scale mile of 70 feet in this time, a rate of 87.5 feet per second. In other words, still an actual 60 m.p.h. .... Oh dear!

This is where I upset the slide-rule merchants by asserting that the above proves that there's more to creating a convincing illusion on a model railway than the mere application of linear maths. As with so many aspects of the craft, selecting an appropriate speed for your trains is a case of making a judgement - of arriving at something that looks right to you. Hopefully, others will then also find it convincing. If they choose to take issue on the matter, then the same rule that applies in all such subjective situations comes into force. That's the one that says 'it's my train set, so...'

CHAPTER 4

Planning and Presentation

Formats and footprints

I've expounded on my use of these terms before, but for the sake of clarity and consistency I'll re-visit my definitions again here, as these are both useful layout-design concepts and hence design tools. The format is how I describe the nature of the basic precept of the layout - continuous run, end-to-end, terminus-to-fiddleyard, fiddleyard-to-fiddle-yard and out-and-back are all formats. However, each of these formats may in turn be accomplished in different ways depending upon how they're arranged on the site. So island, circular, round the walls, linear shelf, L-shaped shelf, peninsula, multi-peninsula, folded, dogbone, teardrop or vertically staged are all possible footprints. Or, put another way, layout shapes.

In some cases, the two concepts are immutably linked. You can't reasonably put an continuous run on a linear shelf foot-print, while it wouldn't make a lot of sense to try and arrange an end-to-end or out-and-back design on a circular footprint. But many formats can use a number of different footprints; continuous runs, for instance, don't have to be ovals, circles or ellipses; they can be dogbones, folded, stacked or L-shaped, or even multi-peninsula (a very common arrangement in the USA). End-to-end formats can also be accommodated on a number of footprints, some less than obvious - the peninsula or teardrop, for example. Where space is tight and ambitions grand, it's often a slightly 'lateral' take on the combination of format and footprint that can save the day. To aid the thought processes a little, I've sketched some typical footprints here.

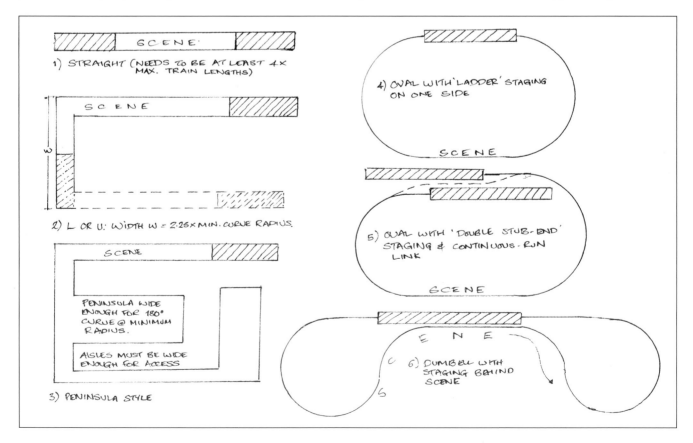

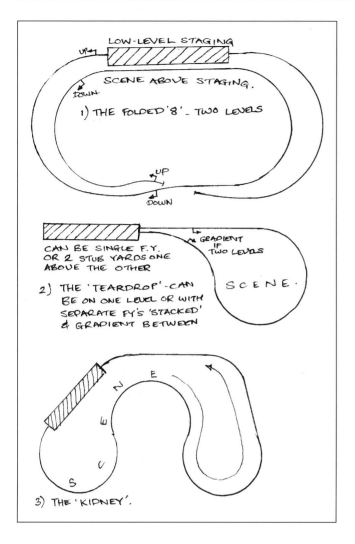

There's no arguing that some footprints are more applicable to certain sites and formats than others - especially in a main line context. I'm not saying that one can't build end-to-end or fiddleyard-scenic section-fiddleyard straight-line or L-shaped main lines, but they have some pretty fundamental drawbacks. With a median train length of around seven foot six in 4mm scale, and assuming that one wishes the train to be able to run through the scenic part of the layout for at least its own length rather than fitting it exactly, this suggests a minimum end-to-end distance of four times the train length, or at least thirty feet - of which half will be hidden fiddleyard. This is neither a very compact sort of footprint nor a good use of precious space. But if you bend it around and join the ends, things immediately look a lot more manageable. The good old oval takes some beating....

The classic oval

An oval of track with a loop on one side and a siding on the other, on which the statutory Pacific and two coaches lapped endlessly at near-warp speeds, is the archetypal 'trainset' format for a minimal main-line layout, usually nailed down to a one-

piece six-by-four baseboard painted bright green. Compact it may have been (although a far-from-rigid six-by-four baseboard made of hardboard panel-pinned to an insubstantial framework is actually a pretty unwieldy object), but a footprint for a realistic model railway it ain't. These days, such things are largely regarded as obsolete and inappropriate even for trainsets - although the American equivalent, the ubiquitous four-by-eight, is still popular. Given that to work around such a layout you need a clear site area of eight by twelve (to allow a two-foot-wide access all round) this has long struck me as anachronistic. A shelf-type around-the-walls footprint on the same size of site offers a far wider range of possibilities.

But some version of the classic continuous-run oval is still the most usually-appropriate and popular format for a main-line layout. The basic design then comes down to accommodating the biggest continuous-run footprint that'll fit the space, and hiding the fact that the trains are merely galloping around in circles - which means we still need an 'offstage' area. The advantage of the widely-used oval (or, preferably, ellipse) with the modelled scene on one side linked to a fiddleyard on the opposite side are severalfold. Firstly, one fiddleyard can serve both 'ends' of the layout; secondly, somewhere around two-thirds of the linear length of the model are usually available for 'scenicing' or display purposes; more, with a bit of boxing clever or use of alternate fiddleyard locations. Thirdly, several styles or formats can be allowed for and incorporated on the oval-based layout. And fourthly, just because you've got a continuous run doesn't mean you have to operate as such - more prototypical and realistic approaches are quite possible. Although I'd never underestimate the advantage of having a track on which things can be allowed to stretch their legs and just circulate; apart from being a pleasant diversion when you're not inclined to give prototypical operation the attention it needs, the chance to really settle down and run does wonders for your locomotives.

The oval in some form is also a very efficient use of a given space, especially if the fiddleyard is arranged either beneath or in parallel with the running lines. It's often said that oval layouts are inherently unrealistic, but I don't agree this is necessarily the case. For a start, if it's an around-the-walls oval and you're sitting in the middle of it you can't see the whole thing in one go. And there's no law that says that it must be presented as one continuous scene (on which point, more in a moment). In fact, the basic more-or-less oval footprint is immensely versatile and offers scope for a wider range of potential track layouts, formats and presentational options than almost any other. In a small space, it's usually unbeatable.

Linear layouts

The straight or L-shaped linear footprint is the other staple of the British layout tradition - although more usually associated with the station-centred layout - often a minor terminus, but sometimes a through type fed by a pair of fiddleyards. In a main-line context, a linear layout will usually require a site offering scope for a 'long thin' footprint of some sort - the popular American ideal of the 'multi-peninsula' footprint is a way of packing a lot of linear run into a rectangular space of some sort. Peninsulas are only part of the story, however; they need to be separated by aisles, which in turn need to wide enough for comfortable operation. Curve radii, too, need to be allowed for, all of which means that the linear/peninsula type of footprint is really only practicable on a larger site.

One linear form which does have quite a lot to commend it is the U-shape, where a narrow shelf runs around the perimeter of a larger space such as a garage. This has the advantage of leaving much of the space unencumbered and hence available for other purposes. I have designed such layouts very much as part of the domestic environment, as a low-impact secondary use of larger room having some other main function, while quite often it can reconcile the needs of the trains and the car in the garage situation.

Fiddleyards - the necessary evil

On the very model of a modern model railway, the fiddleyard is the key to creating the illusion that what is seen on the model is not the whole story, but is - in fact - merely a part of a far greater whole. The trouble with fiddleyards is that if you're not careful they can all-too-easily hijack the whole show - as with so many aspects of layout design, it's a case of striking the right balance of finding the most apposite configuration. Which is why you'll find that quite a few of these layout designs - even

the oval/continuous run examples - often have somewhat 'odd' double-stub-end or 'stacked' fiddleyards, when it may have seemed simpler (and perhaps preferable) to use a conventional double-ended ladder.

The problem with ladders is the old one of length. In the context of a main line in a modest space, we're actually setting out to make the problem more intractable by effectively opting to combine a relatively long train with a space which will invariably be too short. There are certain things on model railways that can be fiddled and compressed, but there are many more which are unfortunately immutable. Which inconveniences include the length of a locomotive or a piece of stock, or a turnout of a given radius. Which means that, no matter how short the site, the length needed to arrange a turnout and enough 'lead' to give clearance between trains of a length of 'loco + x vehicles' on adjacent tracks can only be cut down to the limits dictated by the radius of curvature over which the stock will operate. Although I'll also point out that it'll be less in 00 than in EM or P4, simply because a 00 turnout is shorter by the factor by which the gauge is underscale, which cuts down the 'lead' needed to get a diverging road from the tip of the blades to the nose of the crossing. This factor is actually more significant than you might imagine - a 16.5mm gauge 1 in 6 turnout is a good inch shorter than the P4 equivalent. Which in turn means that if you're talking a multi-track ladder involving several such turnouts, the difference can soon add up to six or eight inches - quite enough to be the deciding factor between 'just fits' and 'won't go'.

Viewpoint has a lot to do with the perception of track gauge. This layout, built by Norman Solomons, uses Peco Streamline 00 track, but is displayed at eye level, so that the viewer looks across the track, not down on it. Combined with clever painting and weathering of the track itself, the result is full of atmosphere and more convincing than many a 'fine scale' model. *Author.*

The Train Stacker fiddleyard

This is really a vertical version of the traditional traverser with the 'table' carrying track on shelves sliding up and down, rather than a ladder of tracks sliding sideways. It was inspired by the Anderton boat-lift that connects the River Weaver with the Trent and Mersey canal, within sight of which I resided one student summer while on a holiday job. It also has much in common with the common-or-garden Victorian sash window. In 4mm scale, the vertical headroom needed between tracks is a minimum of 2.25", so the 3-inch shelf separation proposed here gives room to spare. Using double-track shelves 3-inches wide, the six-foot-long stacker in the drawing could handle ten six-coach trains in an area only about six inches wide by 30-inches of total vertical travel.

The actual train-carrier is based on a sheet of stout ply about 1/2" thick, to which the track-carrying shelves are firmly attached. This slides in a guide frame based on a further sheet of ply - which keeps everything square, and to which are fixed the support uprights. Ideally, this guide frame wants to be hung from a wall, but the whole thing could be made free-standing if necessary with suitable extra framingg; it's essential that it is accurately upright and maintains its accuracy in square if you don't want your stacker to jam in the guides. The support uprights need to be substantial (2 x 2 timber or similar), screwed and glued firmly in place and exactly parallel.

These support uprights carry the guides - I used channel-section plastic drawer-runner strip (B & Q et al), with a pair of upright bearers at either end of the train carrier being fitted with the plastic guide blocks that run in this channel. On top of each support upright is a pulley for the 'sash' counterbalance arrangement; the sort of plastic wheels sold by DIY shops - minus the tyres - are ideal for this. The actual counterweights are made up of something suitably heavy (I used some big old iron nuts on my trial rig) threaded onto the sash-cords, for which I used the real McCoy; it is still available from traditional ironmongers, is very strong and doesn't fray. The idea of the guide track is to locate the carrier fore-and-aft without introducing excessive friction - I found you need a tad of side-to-side play in the track to ensure there are no 'binds'. The counterweights

need to blance the weight of the carrier as far as possible. Obviously, this will change as trains run on and off; I found it best to set things up with one shelf empty and all the others full. Precise balance is not imortant - the system is only there to make the carrier relatively easy to move.

So far so good. The key to the whole ghastly contraption is the locking mechanism, which only permits the carrier to move when it overcome. Various systems will do this job - the arrangement sketched uses a pair of uprights with alignment holes drilled to match the spacing of the shelves. This doesn't call for great precision - the holes are just there to engage with simple plunger-type bolts to ensure that the carrier can't move unintentionally and that it comes to rest somewhere near the correct level in relation to the lead-in tracks when the lock engages; location bolts on the ends of the shelve secure the final alignment, just as on a conventional traverser.

I was rather pleased with the way the locking mehanism worked out. It is based on a pair of drilled upright guide-strips two feet apart - a foot either side of the centre-line - firmly fixed to the ply backing board of the guide frame. Ideally, these guide-strips need a metal facing to avoid wear - I used aluminium angle as drawn. On similar centres are two chunky grab-handles, made of 2 x1 planed timber with the edges radiused off, attached by simple steel strip brackets

to the lowest and uppermost shelves of the carrier. Simple wooden levers screwed to the sides of these grab-handles are linked to the pair of spring-loaded plungers which - in this case - fit under the centre shelf of the five-shelf carrier. But any shelf somewhere near the vertical centreline would do. With a 3-inch shelf separation, there's enough clearance for this mechanism not to interfere with the trains on the tracks beneath. My trial rig used plungers concocted from Meccano rod and screw-on collars, loaded with a couple of stiffish compression coil springs from one of those big bags of mixed springs that Proops used to sell for £1. Any more-or-less and similar compression coil spring will do, or you could use tension spings working the other way round..

To operate the stacker, you grasp both handles and press the levers firmly with your thumbs; this withdraws the bolts from the holes in the guides on the backing plate and allows the carrier to move up or down . As soon as the plunger is free of the hole, the levers are released and the plunger will then drop into the hole for the next level with a resounding 'thunk'. The travel on the plungers doesn't need to be great - half and inch is plenty, as the drawer track at each end of the carrier provides accurate vertical alignment and with the counterbalance arrangement taking most of the weight, you're not placing any great load on the plungers.

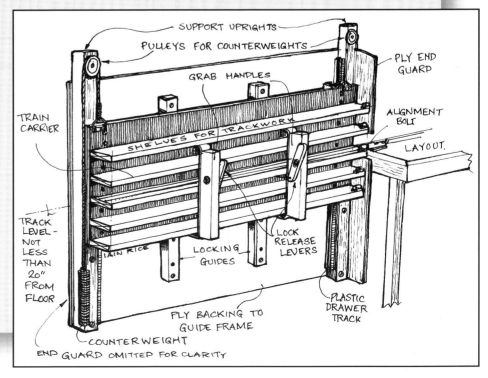

SUPPORT UPRIGHTS
PULLEYS FOR COUNTERWEIGHTS
PLY END GUARD
GRAB HANDLES
TRAIN CARRIER
ALIGNMENT BOLT
SHELVES FOR TRACKWORK
LAYOUT.
TRACK LEVEL - NOT LESS THAN 20" FROM FLOOR
IAIN RICE
LOCKING GUIDES
LOCK RELEASE LEVERS
PLASTIC DRAWER TRACK
PLY BACKING TO GUIDE FRAME
COUNTERWEIGHT
END GUARD OMITTED FOR CLARITY

The other traditional answer to minimum-length fiddle-yards on continuous runs has been the traverser. These can work very well, but the snag is that in traditional horizontal format they need plenty of width if they are going to have a reasonable number of roads. Where double tracks are involved, very accurate track alignment and locking is also required to make sure both running lines always align with a traverser track. But it's that width requirement that often rules it out in the context of a minimum-space mainline, as the result will tend to be an unacceptable tightening of curve radii on the running lines. My own slightly radical solution to this particular conundrum is illustrated alongside - the 'train stacker' or 'vertical traverser'. This is not as difficult to make as it might appear and is no more difficult to align than a convention horizontal traverser, sector plate or cassette. My own design of 'stacker' runs on either drawer track or sliding door gear and uses sash-window type counterweights to make it relatively easy to move. There's a fail-safe braking system to stop it doing any dramatic downward plunges, and a good tight-fitting bolt is as effective an alignment/securing device in this application as it is in more conventional sliding fiddleyards.

Presentation

This is one of Rice's favourite hobby-horses, and hence was bound to come trotting along before long - in this case, with very good reason. To those who find themselves pursing their lips in disapproval when I advocate the adoption of impure 00 for some applications (such as most of those considered here), I would like to pose a question: What is it about 00 that

makes it look odd and so obviously wrong? Yes, the gauge is too narrow and the overhangs hence too great. And yes, the flangeways through pointwork are wider than they should be - although, these days, usually no worse than EM. The same, in fact. Which leads on to a further pertinent question: When does one most notice these anomalies? Correct: When looking down on the layout from above - as one so often is where traditional 'table top' display height is used.

But what if, instead of looking down on the modelled scene, one looks across it more-or-less at eye level? Yes, the head-on view is still compromised - but that's not the apparent one where the trains are essentially passing through the field of view from side-to-side. Looking across trackage and trains at right angles to this direction, neither the underscale gauge nor the overscale flangeways are particularly evident. It's things like the wheels, the below-footplate detail and the quality of the valve gear that impinge. Which, given the standard of modern RTR, simply isn't a problem, at least in 4mm scale. In fact, in this situation, it's extremely difficult to differentiate between 00 and EM.

This observation is in no way meant to denigrate the finer standards. Rather, it is an attempt to put them in context and to suggest a way of reducing the impact of compromised standards adopted - in the cause of pragmatism - for reasons already explored. Using eye level display for the layout minimises the impact of these and other compromises, such as over-tight curve radii. There are other plus points - quite small scenic features or structures, for instance - are sufficient to act as 'view blocks', hiding or distracting the eye from other bits of

More recent RTR doesn't incorporate the sort of give-aways that often characterised older models when viewed close-up or on eye level. This is a Bachmann (née Mainline) Jubilee, whose worst fault is undersized cylinders; it was a useful and straightforward improvement to fit scale-sized Comet cast/etched cylinders in their place, together with some nicer bogie wheels from Alan Gibson. *Author's Collection.*

pragmatism that might otherwise intrude. And, of course, the viewpoint is the natural one when viewing the trains 'from the lineside'. Watching John Huntley's film-clips of trains on video, one is struck by how often a low camera angle is used to emphasise the drama and impact of a passing express.

However, eye-level display is not a universal panacea. Really, it is most relevant to 4mm scale, as this is the ratio which most equates to the 'watching from the lineside' view. The fact that modern 4mm also uses a relatively fine wheel standard, has a range of unobtrusive coupling devices and is big enough to offer concealed mechanisms (no cabs full of motors or whirring armatures visible behind the wheels, to cite two common failings of older 4mm RTR and many 'scale' models). It's also big enough to enable models to carry plenty of detail which modern manufacturing techniques make possible, and to have a fine quality of finish, things which also make it work well in this context.

2mm scale, on the other hand, equates to a more distant view, and lends itself more to the 'panoramic' approach, while the individual models - good though they are - can't stand up to the sort of close-up scrutiny that 4mm can (and 7mm excels at). In the case of N, particularly - with its still somewhat 'chunky' wheel profile, obtrusive coupler and generally less refined detail and finish - the close-up eye-level view does it few favours. The strength of 2mm is its ability to depict the railway in the landscape, and to recreate the experience of, say, sitting on a sunny hillside and watching the trains pass in the valley below. Which requires a rather different type of presentation, more suited to recreating this 'distant, slightly elevated' viewpoint. So I prefer to site N scale a little way below eye level but - and here's the important bit - with a backscene that encapsulates a natural horizon line and which hence extends to above eye level. Only then can one capture the effect of looking out over a real landscape rather than down at a model.

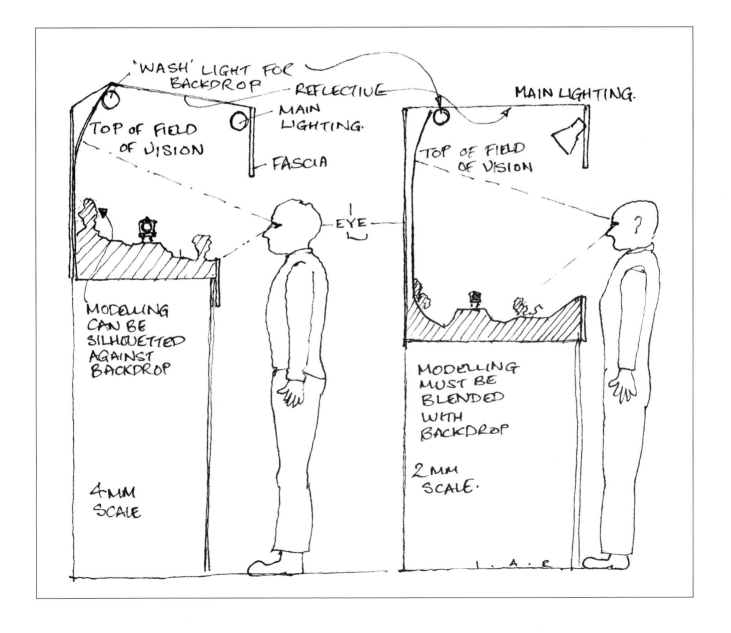

Track Layouts and train working

When designing model railways, there are lots of temptations to 'improve' the prototype in terms of 'ease of working'. And yes, I'll put my hand up and plead 'guilty' to many such lapses in the murk of my own modelling past. We're all familiar with the impossibly tidy country station, the 'prize length' coal siding and other such bits of unrealistic idealism in the 'look' of layouts. But what also seems to have grown up is a tradition of track layout design that sets out to make everything as straightforward as possible. There are scores of layouts that are composed entirely of straight left- and right-hand turnouts, all of the same radius/angle, all laid out in an artificially regular alignment that shuns reverse curves, subtle deviations or things out of parallel. There has also seemed to be an imperative to avoid at any cost curves of varying radii, complex point formations, setting-back moves, contrary shunts and other such quirks.

A lot of real railway working and track layout design, on the other hand, is characterised by just such awkwardnesses, of ways of going about things that strike one as decidedly perverse in a model railway context. Well, perverse they may appear, but chances are that there were very good reasons for such apparent quirks. Often, these reasons are arcane, in that they have to do with Board of Trade regulations, internal company policies, the preferences and prejudices of generations of civil, PW and signal engineers, and the hugely complex nature of the operating pattern. Both locomotives and stock were intensively rostered, and many an apparently-inexplicable manoeuvre was determined by the need to make power, rolling stock or track space available for workings quite other than the one actually being contemplated. But probably the over-riding factor in all matters of track layout design, especially in respect of main running lines, were the complex and intractable requirements of the Board of Trade. Britain's railways were among the most closely-regulated and lavishly-equipped in the world. They were also just about the safest.

In terms of track layout design on main running lines, it all came down to the facing point. This was the great no-no, and was avoided unless absolutely indispensable - when it was protected by locking mechanisms, speed limits and other measures. But if one really looks at a great many 'inexplicable' bits of track layout design, it is then apparent that facing points in running lines are much, much rarer on the prototype than they are on models. And it's also apparent that a lot of the 'odd' workings (and there are several such described in the various proposals later in this book) were due to the need to avoid 'facing' moves. The result may look awkward and odd, and one often studies a prototype track plan and thinks 'Why didn't they just bung in a crossover here?' or 'Why is that only a single slip and not a double?' The reason is almost invariably that these would have introduced facing connections, which had to be justified to the Railway Inspectorate. And

Inspectorate's the policy was to restrict such P & C work to the totally unavoidable. So, surely, should we?

But many a model railway has a track layout and operating practices that would never have satisfied a Board of Trade Railway Inspector. Why is this? Well, for a start, lack of know-how; the mainstream model railway tradition evolved from the trainset/toy end of things rather than from the prototype. But I suspect that it was largely because in the past, when component quality was not that great and the importance of standards was not as well-appreciated as it is today, many of the operations performed routinely on the real railways - such as setting back through crossovers and shunting around reverse curves - were fraught with difficulty on a model. It wasn't until the advent of fine scale standards (often decried as 'impossible' not so very long ago!) and the much more rigorous approach to both the wheel/track interface and things like proper track geometry, accurately-aligned buffers and more sophisticated coupling systems that it became possible to contemplate many of these manoeuvres. Today, refinements like suspension or compensation of stock, consistent weighting, free-running pinpoint bearings and much better matching of wheel and track standards across the board have largely eliminated the old bugbears of unreliable trackholding and buffer-locking. So, I'd argue, it is no longer necessary to 'cook the books' in terms of track layout and working practice. So I haven't.

Operational philosophy

This is something that has never figured over-large in discussions of layout design on these shores (although it'll while away whole evenings and bottle after bottle of knock-kneed beer the other side of the Atlantic). There are a number of reasons for this, I feel, starting with the fact that our far more modest layouts don't provide a huge amount of operational scope when compared with the sort of basement-busting empire so many US modellers aspire to. Be that as it may, I think that closer attention to the Modus Operandi is perhaps overdue on these shores; I've lost count of the number of highly-realistic looking model railways I've seen on which utterly unrealistic forms of operation are practised. And yup, I've been guilty of just such sins myself in the past; but there's no-one like a zealous convert for a bit of evangelising!

My conclusion is that you can approach the operation of a model railway from two basic viewpoints, which I've christened the 'inside' and 'outside' perspectives. The difference lies in the objective of actually operating the layout in the first place: is it to replicate and meet the challenges faced by professional railwaymen in running a real train service on a real railway - the 'inside' approach - or is it simply to provide a parade of trains to keep spectators 'outside' the lineside fence enter-

The prototype sometimes seems quite perverse in the way it does things. Here is an M & GN 'J3' 0-6-0 shunting at Spalding; the tracks to the right of the train are the platform loop road and the (GN/GE) down main line to Doncaster. No facing points anywhere!

H C Casserley/*Author's Collection.*

tained? I'd suggest that in Britain, where the exhibition is King and a large proportion of model railways - especially larger main-line-themed ones - are essentially designed for display purposes, the latter is almost always the case. Whereas in the US, where portable layouts are as common as mountaineers in Kansas, the opposite is usually true.

I'm not suggesting that we should all go in for US style intensive by-the-rule-book operation; apart from all other considerations, the very different prototypical operating practices mean that the American approach is not really very relevant in a British context. When you try and explain to a US modeller that Britain's railways are fully signalled on the absolute block system, they look at you in amazement; they are used to hundreds and hundreds of miles of unsignalled single track controlled by nothing more sophisticated than a dispatcher issuing written train orders that are passed to the train crew by much the same process as token exchange on a single-track British branch.

Be that as it may, I do think that we loose a whole aspect of railway modelling by abandoning any semblance of prototypical operation in favour of the ubiquitous 'control panel', where one or two people - seated behind banks of switches and coloured lights that often look more like the mission centre for Star Wars than anything to do with a railway - control every aspect of the layout. Even in reality, in these days of area signalling schemes and CTC, we still have the essential divide between those who drive the trains and those who direct them. In steam-era terms, we have engine drivers and signalmen; and it's the core of the whole prototype operating philosophy that these two functions are entirely separate. My own feeling is that this is a fundamental of British railway practice that well repays incorporation into layout design, and nowhere more so than in the context of a main line layout. The advent of Digital Command Control (DCC) also gives us a powerful new tool to use in this quest for operational authenticity.

Control design

Some people apparently like those huge control panels with lots of switches, knobs and lights. I just find them confusing. I also find that they don't convey a very railway-like 'feel' to the process of running a layout. Show me a model railway with proper lever frames, full signalling and trains driven using loco controls that are not only separate from the signalling/route setting functions but which also approximate to the function of driving a real train - then you're talking! Nowadays, all the necessary components for this type of operation are available 'off the shelf', and if you haven't yet tried operating using such a system, I'd urge you to give it a go. Combine the aesthetic joys of realistic model trains with a mental stimulus akin to chess!

Although I suppose it would be possible to arrange a traditional centralised panel for any of the schemes proposed here, that isn't what I had in mind when I was designing them. At the very least, I would envisage a clear separation between the signalling/route-setting function and the train-driving. If possible, these days I'd do the second part by DCC, not just because it does away with a whole tier of wiring - the track power sections - but because it offers a far better and more convincing way of 'driving' model trains. Not only is the locomotive being 'driven' (admittedly remotely) by an onboard system, but DCC offers a unique level of individual control. You have the chance to select and 'tune' each chip to suit the locomotive it's installed in - effectively giving you a customised and optimised controller for every engine on the layout. Or, put another way, equivalent to having a crew skilled in getting the best from that particular engine on the footplate.

Most DCC systems offer a lot more than this. Some, indeed, offer rather too much. I'm not convinced by the use of the 'driving' digital system for point and signal control, as you end up back with the same over-centralised set-up as the old-fashioned control panel. Digital point and signal control, yes - but in the context of a system based on a lever frame/instrument set that replicated the role of the signalman rather than as an add-on to the driver's system. My ideal DCC system would offer a compact handheld (and preferably wireless - both radio and infra-red based schemes are available in the USA) unit for the driver of each locomotive, a unit which offered only the basic tools of his trade: regulator, reverser and brakes. All other functions would be managed from the 'signal box' panel(s), including programming and train allocation.

The other exciting prospect offered by DCC is realistic onboard sound. Like a lot of British finescale modellers, I was initially very sceptical about the value of this in the context of 'serious' railway modelling, but having now gained experience with the SoundTrax system in the USA I'm convinced that it adds a whole new dimension to the realistic operation of model railways. I await the introduction of a British system with impatience. It's going to need a bit of further miniaturisation before all the gubbins will fit into a typical British 0-6-0 tank, but the dawn of a new and sonorous day cannot be far off!

Even without DCC, however, there is considerable scope for introducing a far more prototypical style of operation on layouts like those proposed here. The bugbear of track section switches can be circumvented by using the signalling circuits to feed power to the running lines, while I have used hand-held controllers and separate signalling panels for years. Now that a choice of very nice lever frames is available for either mechanical or electric actuation of points and signals (or a combination of both), then I can see no reason for accepting a control system that is nothing more than an a collection of mere common-or-garden toggle switches. Even if - for reasons of space or economy - these must be used, why not bank them as a lever frame and colour-code them accordingly? It's the least you can do....

Balance

There are a whole range of other factors to take account of when considering standards and design criteria for a new layout, but the fundamental objective is surely to arrive at a balanced and satisfying result. Which would not, I'd suggest, consist of a superdetailed professionally built and painted Finney loco pulling a train of Triang 'shorty' coaches through technicolour sawdust scenery past structures made from Bilteezi cards. Far better to settle for a good modern RTR loco and some matching stock, and concentrate on getting everything else to the same standard...

All of which is by way of suggesting that, exciting though the apparent possibilities opened up by the development of ever-more refined and sophisticated standards and techniques for ultra hi-fidelity fine scale railway modelling are, these things also have their price and their place - and that, in many instances, something less than the ultimate that is technically possible may actually serve your purposes better. Such is frequently the case with the domestic main-line layout, where I feel that good quality 00 used to its best advantage is a better solution than badly compromised P4. And on this supposition I have based the proposals presented in this book.

CHAPTER 5

Modest Main Line Plans
introduction

The fourteen layouts drawn and described in this section range - hopefully - across a broad spectrum of subject, scale and space. As is usual with these books, these are all layouts which I could - with my hand on my heart - say that I would be happy to build. Some of them, indeed, are true favourites, which I would dearly like to take a crack at, if ever I have a little more railway modelling real-estate at my disposal: Melling, Bodmin Road and Wickham Market are all high on my (admittedly lengthy) 'wish-list'.

Rather than reworking all these designs into a uniform format, they are presented here 'as drawn' - some as simple pencil sketches, some as pen and ink line drawings and a few in water-colour. They are mostly drawn freehand, so any wonky lines are down to advancing age! It's always a difficult judgement as to how much information one should try and include on a plan of this type, but I do like my detail and I just hope that things still remain clear enough. I have developed a little library of symbols/abbreviations that I tend to use and these are set out in the panel here. I think several are conventions in general use, but I think many of them are more familiar in the USA than here.

These layouts are, of course, simply proposals, examples or suggestions. If anybody builds one of these efforts 'verbatim', I'll be as surprised as I am flattered! But hopefully, there will be subject ideas, configurations and practical arrangements here that will find wider applications, or maybe suggest original lines of enquiry or possible solutions to existing problems. With railway modelling, as in wider life, it's usually a case of "where there's a will, there's some way or other."

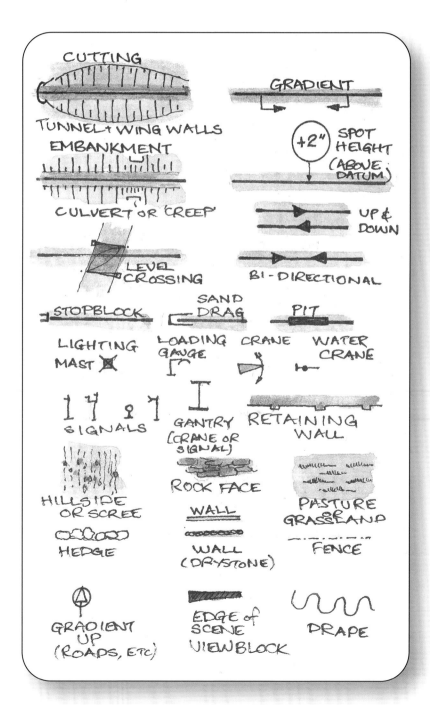

Luxulyan

I'm going to start this selection of main-line layout suggestions off with what is, strictly speaking, a cheat. For the dramatic section of railway from Par to Newquay is not, technically, a main line at all - normally being referred to as the Newquay branch. Well yes - in terms of precise definition, it is. But in terms of ambience and the sort of trains one could see toiling over it, it had some very 'main line' characteristics. If by 'branch' we understand some quiet rural byway, then the Newquay line was the very antithesis of that. Rural byways didn't host through trains from all over Britain, call for double-heading with banking, or the use of some of the largest and most powerful types of diesel locomotives to run on our national network.

The Newquay line is certainly rural, in that it runs for something over 20 miles through a verdant (if somewhat despoiled) countryside, and serves few places of any importance en route. But its terminus is a hugely popular holiday destination, one of Cornwall's premier resorts that attracts tens of thousands of visitors every year. It may not be Blackpool, but some of the trains that toiled up from Par to the heights of Goss Moor over what had started life as a mere mineral line were pretty substantial, and even today there are still a few long-distance through trains serving the resort. In steam days, scheduled express trains loading to twelve or more packed coaches and arriving from a number of far-flung points of origin were the order of the day, and posed a fair challenge to the operating department.

The Newquay line might technically be a single track branch, but it had a fearsome gradient fit to equal the steepest found on any main line - 1 in 37, the same as dreaded Dainton or the fabled Lickey Incline. Worse, the section of line up through the beautiful Luxulyan valley didn't just climb, it twisted and turned around a series of sharp reverse curves that increased the problem, while the bank was approached, not by some stretch of favourable line permitting a charge, but by a difficult traverse of the busy St Blazey yards followed by a mile or so of straight-and-level - which is then quite spoiled by a twisting section through Ponts Mill at the foot of the bank proper.

Working heavy passenger traffic up such a route has always called for full-blooded measures, and in steam days a fifteen-coach high-season summer working posed a challenge met with the dramatic combination of a pair of main-line 4-6-0s on the head end with a Prairie tank or mogul shoving hard in the rear. Being a main line in terms of infrastructure and axle loading, all the principal classes working into Cornwall ran on up to Newquay - Castles, Counties, Halls, Granges and Manors, together with Moguls, small and large Prairie tanks and, of course, plethora of pannier tanks on china-clay workings. With the arrival of the first-generation Western Region diesel hydraulics, nothing much changed in that it usually needed at least two or three (sometimes more!) of these to stagger up the bank with a holiday train - and stagger they did! Only with the arrival of the 'Western' 2,700 hp Co-Co type and the second-generation BR designs such as classes 47 and, most notably, class 50, did double heading up the hill become less than commonplace. Since late 1987, all through workings have been in the form of 'cross country' HST sets - which arrived at Newquay from as far afield as Scotland. With 5,500 h.p. available to haul less than ten coaches, these usually manage the climb without problem!

The early 1980s were a great time on the Luxulyan Valley route. Yes, we had lost steam power, but a full range of main-line diesel types could be seen (and heard!) working all-out around those curves: Westerns, 47s, 50s, Peaks, EE Type 4s, almost everything bar a Deltic. The china-clay trains rated a pair of sparkling 'Cornish Railways' 37s, or were hauled by any type from that eclectic mix of main-line types, filling-in between passenger turns. Only the local passenger workings descended to the drudgery of DMUs - usually the type 121 or the single-unit class 122 'bubble cars' . Today, the regular service is worked by the ubiquitous Regional Railways 2-car 'Pacer' sets, after a disastrous dalliance with the 4-wheeled class 142 'Skippers' - which had relatively little power and no sanding gear. A great idea for a heavily-graded route in a damp climate!

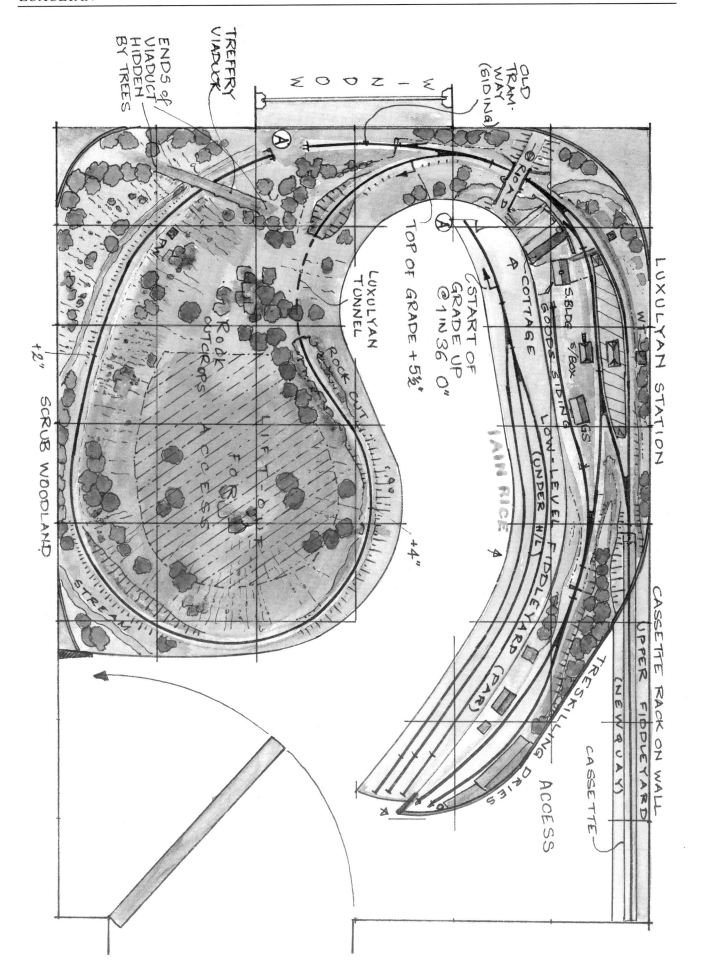

WIND-DOW

OLD TRAM-WAY (SIDING)

ENDS of VIADUCT HIDDEN BY TREES

TREFFRY VIADUCT

A

START OF GRADE UP @ 1 IN 36 0"

TOP OF GRADE +5½"

A

LUXULYAN TUNNEL

ROCK CUT

(N) ROCK OUTCROPS

LIFT-OUT FOR ACCESS

+4"

+2"

SCRUB WOODLAND

STREAM

ROAD

COTTAGE

S.BLDG

S/Box

GS

MAIN RICE

GOODS SIDING

LOW-LEVEL FIDDLE YARD (UNDER H/L)

LUXULYAN STATION

TRESKILLING DRIES

CASSETTE RACK ON WALL

UPPER FIDDLE YARD (NEW QUAY)

CASSETTE

TRESKILLING ACCESS

A down Newquay express leaving Newton Abbot in 1950, behind 'Monmouth Castle' (with Hawksworth tender);
these were the largest engines to work up the Luxulyan valley. *Author's Collection.*

Luxulyan in miniature

This layout proposal based on the Newquay branch in the period 1980 -1990 is an old favourite of mine, and is one of the few N gauge layouts I've ever got close to building. I even acquired a Farish class 37 and an HST set in readiness, so I must have been serious! It fulfils a number of my criteria for a suitable subject in a very modellogenic setting and is also, I feel, well suited both to N scale and the 'panoramic' approach. The Luxulyan valley is very much one of those places where one sits on the hillside to watch the trains toil up those sinuous curves beneath.

I've chosen a somewhat-unusual footprint for this compact design intended for an eight-by-six 'third bedroom' or garden-shed site. I call this shape the 'extended teardrop', and it's a configuration I have used successfully in both a US and a European context. Basically, it's only suited to modelling gradients and banks - which makes it ideal in this case - and saves space by 'stacking' a pair of fiddle-yards directly one above the other, with the scenic section linking the two. In this case, the upper fiddleyard is hidden behind a 'signature' foreground industry, the Treskilling clay dries, which in turn is sited above the lower fiddleyard.

I'll confess straight away that I've taken all sorts of temporal and topographical liberties in concocting this scheme. The Treskilling Dries just mentioned closed long before a Class 50 or an HST ever heaved itself up the hill, and the geographical order of things in the ascent of the valley has been re-arranged somewhat to fit the space. My chief objective has been to capture the essence of the sinuous single track threading the valley floor, crossed - of course - by the greatest signature item on the whole line, the magnificent granite 1843 Treffry viaduct/aqueduct. Other Luxulyan Valley 'layout design elements' included are the steep valley-sides covered with scrub woodland and punctuated with rock outcrops, the curving rock cutting leading to the short (52-yard) Luxulyan tunnel, and Luxulyan station itself.

This last had, by the mid-1980s, been reduced to a single track past a weed-grown platform complete with 'bus shelter', replacing the earlier GWR Pagoda hut. But Luxulyan had for most of its life been a passing place, and with the growth of the Newquay passenger traffic boasted an island platform in the loop and the station building off to one side - another signature of these ex-CMR (Cornwall Minerals Railway) lines. In former times, Luxulyan also had a goods yard which housed, for many years, a camping coach. It will come as no surprise that in this scheme, the loop, signal box and station building have 'survived' - well, with Treskilling Dries still open, run-round facilities are essential, are they not? And yes, I do realise that the access to the dries should trail off the goods yard headshunt rather than being a facing connection. And yes, the loop is far too short. But I still feel it captures the essence of the place.

In terms of presentation, this design is a little unusual in that one of the main views - that 'down' the valley towards a distant glimpse of the Treffry Viaduct (which could be modelled as a one side only cut-out, maybe a tad underscale to 'force' the perspective) is seen only from the 'end on' direction. But this does, I feel, capture the essence of this unique location, where the train 'boxes the compass' on the way up the hill. To make this rear area accessible for modelling and maintenance, the entire centre 'hill' of the valley scene lifts out - shown hatched on the plan. I make big lift-outs like this from laminations of expanded polystyrene floor insulation - light, strong and very rigid.

Otherwise, this is actually quite a simple layout to build. The Peco Code 55 N scale trackwork range would provide all that was needed while looking about as good as commercial N scale track can look; ballast it carefully with a really fine material like silver sand. The curves are tight - 18" limiting radius - which should look as flange-grindingly severe as the real thing without causing any problems for N scale equipment. Operation is the parade of traffic up and down the bank, with a spot of shunting at the revived Treskilling Dries to add a little variety. Not a bad recipe for 48 square feet, I feet...

As for the trains - well, you can go from tired Westerns and Warships in the early 1980s to HSTs by 1988. Farish's diesels - classes 37, 47 and 50 - are pretty good models and powerful to boot, so should manage the hill OK. Farish also do a DMU which, while not quite right, (it's a 131, I think) doesn't look out of place. The line also received regular visits from the Chipman weed-killing train, hauled by a class 20; a nice offbeat diversion you don't often see modelled. BR MkII stock for main line workings is no problem, while over the decade timespan of this proposal clay trains went from tradition 'clayhoods' and SWB vans to Polybulks, Tigers and VAA hoppers. Plenty of scope there. Which leaves only those awful couplings to tackle. My own solution is a mix of permanently-coupled rakes of coaches and wagons, with either Kadee or B & B auto-couplers on the locos and the end vehicles.

Summary:
Subject: Br (W) 1980s route to Newquay.
Scale/standards: 2mm N scale or fine scale.
Site: 6 x 8ft spare bedroom or shed.
Max train length: 4 feet.
Limiting curve: 21" radius.
Grade: 1 in 36.

Further Reading:
The Newquay branch and its branches,
by John Vaughan. OPC/Haynes 1991.
The Great western Railway in Mid-Cornwall,
by Alan Bennett, Kingfisher 1988.

The Newquay line in the clay country - a highly characteristic landscape. The main line is on the far right.
Author's Collection.

Barton Staithe
M & GN

Is the M & GN a main line railway? Well, there's a nice debating point! The company certainly considered itself so, and ran a very smart through restaurant-car express service from Melton Constable to Kings Cross (via Peterborough) to prove the point. It also carried a heavy holiday traffic from the East Midlands to the various resorts around the Norfolk and North Suffolk coasts, often by trains that were unequivocally described as 'express'. It had a stud of elegant passenger locomotives, some by Beyer-Peacock, and others of the purest Midland provenance (and none the worse for that!) Some of its train timings were also pretty smart, and 60 m.p.h. was no uncommon speed. What the M & GN didn't have was an impressive multi-track route. Bits of it were double track, certainly - but a great deal more was unremittingly single.

In fact, the M & GN is one of those railways that simply defy convenient classification. It is the polygonal peg that doesn't quite fit any of the usual square or round holes. The

M & GN is a railway enigma, a mass of contradictions in almost its every aspect. It was both progressive and archaic, smart yet dilatory and fiercely independent in spite of being managed by a joint committee. It had main line aspirations with a branchline infrastructure - but built its own locomotives at its own works with all the assured self-sufficiency of a Doncaster or Derby and painted them in a gorgeous livery unlike any other. It served an important city - Norwich - albeit from a rather odd direction, but most of its trackage passed through very rural and sparsely-populated country. And it ran one of the most intensive train services ever to be worked over a single line with aplomb and commendable safety. Accidents on the M & GN were very, very rare. And never serious.

In fact, to work safely an express passenger traffic with some smart timings and 60 mph running speeds over a single line, with automatic tablet exchange on the Whittaker system, required both plant and working practices of a very high

The standard 'cottage' style station of the M & GN makes an attractive prototype for a model.
Author's Collection.

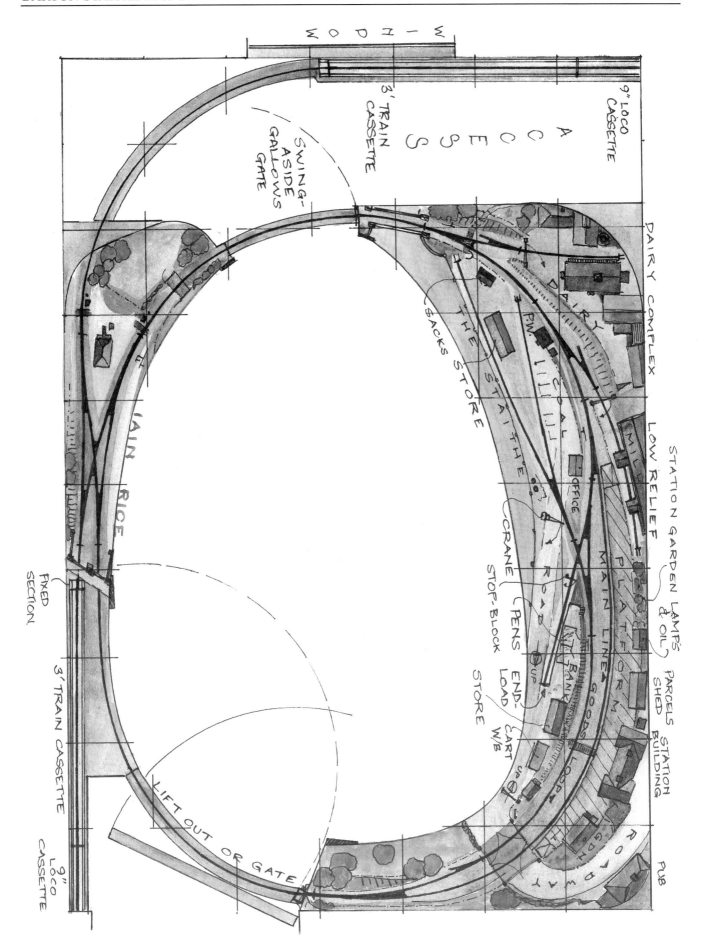

order. But this quest for safety and efficiency did not preclude a due deference to the less formal but undoubtedly appealing aspects of the 'Joint', such as it's charming 'country cottage' stations, with their beautifully-tended gardens and smart Midland-style lattice fencing.

The post-WWII world did not treat the M & GN kindly, at first - in the early to mid 1950s - hopelessly overloading its single-line infrastructure with interminable holiday camp specials and then, when everybody had bought their Ford Anglia or Morris Minor, abandoning it. The fruit and produce

traffic fell also to the so-convenient lorry, and with its seasonal peaks of both passenger and freight traffic dwindling rapidly, the poor old M & GN was left to subsist on the meagre local traffic. It couldn't, of course, and so became one of the first constituents of the nationalised system to be closed more-or-less entirely in one fell swoop, before even the eye of Beeching had lit upon it. A large part of the system died on the last day of February 1959, although freight still ran to Rudham and Norwich and a few other places, while the more important towns like Cromer and Yarmouth retained a

An express of the Midland and Great
Northern Railway on a single-track
section of the route - still a main line!
F Moore postcard/*Author's Collection.*

and a yellow engine, it would seem. And, in truth, it's an ideal subject for a compact layout with main-line aspirations; magnificent its expresses might have been, but they were also blessedly short: a modest 4-4-0 and four or five carriages (some of them six-wheelers) usually sufficed. Perfect! It went on being perfect when most of the others had been swallowed by the 'big four', not finally succumbing to the stifling conformity of take-over by the LNER until October 1936. True, the full flower of the 'Golden Gorse' livery had darkened progressively through ochre to umber and occasional green, but there were still teak carriages and 4-4-0s.

I've seen quite a few models of the M & GN - mostly in 7mm scale - but few which portrayed the railway as anything other than a quaint rural backwater, often almost a light railway. This is far from the picture that emerges when one studies the history of the line - covered by some excellent books - which shows that the 'Joint' was far from bucolic. The permanent way was of high quality and well-maintained - the line's long-serving engineer and manager, Mr William Marriot, holding to the highest standards in such matters. He was also very progressive, pioneering the use of reinforced concrete for structures, signal posts, fencing and even sleepers with integrally-cast chairs.

So these are the aspects of the M & GN that I've set out to try and encapsulate in this modest little layout, which makes somewhat unusual use of the 10 x 7 bedroom site to provide a continuous run with separate cassette fiddleyards facing in both the 'up' and 'down' directions. Otherwise, it's conventional enough fare - a small wayside station. This represents Barton Staithe, an extra stopping place that I've introduced to the south of Horning on the single-track Norfolk and Suffolk joint line down to Yarmouth. Barton Staithe lies on a loop of the river Ant - say I - a mile or two above Barton Broad and a little to the north of Stalham.

This is an attempt to portray an absolutely typical minor wayside station of the M & GN as it would have been in the halcyon years before the first world war, or perhaps shortly afterwards. Barton is a single line block post but not a regular passing place, the loop being provided principally to facilitate working of the goods yard and the two private sidings. It could also be used for passenger trains to overtake slow goods workings, as was regular practice at Caister, a few stops further on towards Yarmouth. The layout is inspired by the arrangements at Hellesdon, on the Norwich line, with a cottage building of the standard (and very

limited passenger service, much of it routed over ex-GE metals. These traffics gradually withered away, and by the end of 1969 only a few short and isolated sections of the old 'Joint' remained in use. RIP.

A model M & GN.

As a subject for modelling, the M & GN is right up there with those other characterful popinjays of the pre-grouping scene, the Brighton, the South Eastern and Chatham, the Caledonian and the Furness; few of us can resist varnished teak coaches

'Gallows' type of swing –
aside layout entry.

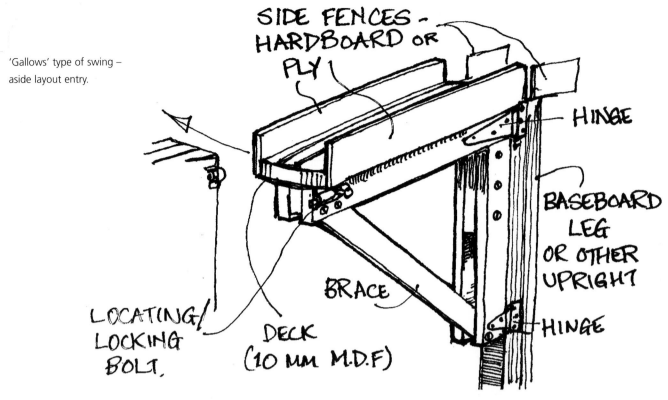

SIDE FENCES -
HARDBOARD OR
PLY

HINGE

BASEBOARD
LEG
OR OTHER
UPRIGHT

HINGE

BRACE

LOCATING/
LOCKING
BOLT.

DECK
(10 MM M.D.F)

comely) design (there are drawings in John Brodribb's 'LNER Country Stations'). The signal box is a GN pattern ridged type (Midland-style hip-roof boxes could also be found), and there is no goods shed as such. These were rare on much of the M & GN.

The other element of the design is the 'Junction' - actually, the entry pointwork to the two fiddleyards - which is vaguely reminiscent of Melton Constable (West) but otherwise is purely fictional and - to be honest about it - geographically unplaced. I just like junctions and this one, with its classic 'single lines doubled at the point of meeting' layout, is a peach. By way of contrast, the cabin here is the MR type, while the signals will, of course, be on cast-concrete bracket posts.

The layout is designed with EM standards in mind, with a limiting curve (on that goods loop) of 2ft 10ins radius - tight, but not too much of a problem for the small 0-6-0s that the M & GN used for goods working. The main line running is all over 3ft radius or a tad more - again, adequate in the context of a modest 4-4-0 and short bogie and six-wheel stock. The M & GN didn't see any 'big' engines until the BR period, which is not at all what I had in mind when designing this layout. Rather, this is an attempt to provide a manageable project for a modeller who wants to build his own locos and stock, with or without the aid of kits. (Alan Gibson has several adaptable candidates in his MR range, as do London Road Models. Falcon Brass have a Hudswell Clarke 4-4-0T and a D class goods.) Fortunately, you won't need a lot of equipment - which is maybe just as well, as you can't get a handy leg-up from Mr Bachmann, or any other RTR maker, if it comes to it.

But, speaking as one who enjoys building locomotives that are neither over large nor over complex, and which

come in such a gorgeous colour scheme, the M & GN is perfect territory. Why, they even had a couple of ex-Cornwall Minerals Railway Sharp Stewart 0-6-0s to make me feel at home! Coaching stock was generally of GN or Midland outline (and often origin), so the usual kit ranges (D & S, Slaters, London Road) covering these railways should provide some grist for the modelling mill. Not a layout project for the faint-hearted or quick-fix modeller, then; but - given a modicum of time, skill and persistence - a rewarding subject for those for whom the constructional journey is as rewarding as the operational arrival.

Summary:

Subject: M & GN around WW I.
Scale/gauge: 4mm/EM.
Site size: 10 x 7 feet.
Ruling curve radius: 34" (goods loop).
Ruling grade: none.
Longest fiddleyard road: 45" cassette - 36" train + 9" loco.

Further reading:

The Midland and Great Northern Joint Railway,
by A J Wrottesly, D & C/1970 (2nd edn 1981).
Scenes from the Midland and Great Northern Joint Railway,
by R H Clarke, Moorland/1978.
Illustrated History of M & GNJR Locomotives,
by R H Clarke. OPC/Haynes 1990.
LNER Country Stations,
by John Brodribb. Ian Allan/1988.

Rowtor

One of the great advantages of hilly scenery is that you can get quite a lot of it into quite a small area - which is very useful attribute in the context of a truly compact layout. And generally, the more precipitous the nature of scenery, the less the horizontal area you need to fit it in. Well, scenery in the British Isles doesn't come any more precipitous than the limestone gorges of the Peak District. That it's also a very modellogenic landscape that was home to some splendidly offbeat railways is almost by way of a bonus.

I spent quite a long time searching for workable minimum-space mainline subjects for 4mm scale, as a restricted site like this 10 x 7 spare bedroom doesn't offer a whole lot of scope. In contrast with my other 4mm offerings on the same site, this is a regular double-track main line although not one noted for high speeds; it's inspired by the Midland's memorable south-east to north-west traverse of the Penines from Derby to Manchester via Matlock, Rowsley, Monsal and Miller's Dales - one of the loveliest and most spectacular routes in England and surely a line that anyone with a grain of forethought would have put at the top of the 'potential tourist line' list. But no - the bottom line is the only line on Britain's railways, and the Midland threads the Peak no more - although several of the more imposing structures are now 'listed'. Thank goodness we still have the Settle and Carlisle.

A number of features make the Midland a great modelling proposition, not least of which was the policy noted in Chapter 3 of running lots of small trains rather than a few big ones - ideal in model railway terms. This seems to have been a policy perpetuated by the LMS and, to a lesser extent, BR, and in researching this design (if I can dignify thumbing through a plethora of books and magazine articles in search of nice inspring pictures with the title 'research') I was struck by the number of trains that were only half-a-dozen coaches long behind the Compound, 'Patriot' or Class 5. In Midland

Pilot engines were often vintage types working out their declining years. LMS No. 15 - an outside-framed Kirtley 6ft 3in 2-4-0, rebuilt by Johnson and dating back to 1870 - was one such. The last of these remarkable engines was not withdrawn until 1947 and one (MR 158A) survives in preservation at the NRM.

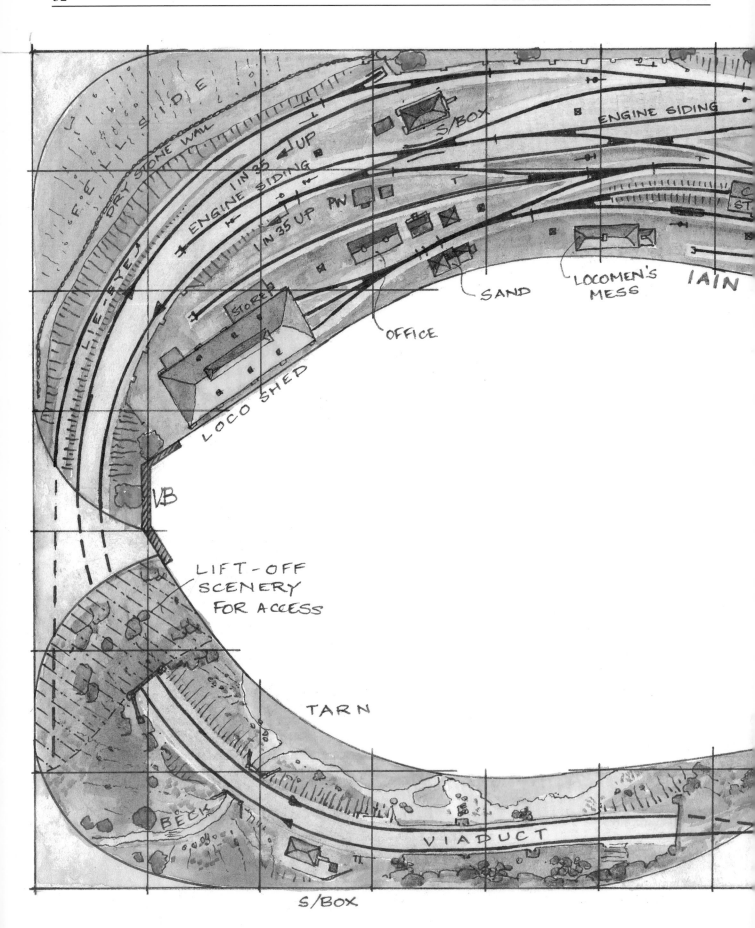

FELLSIDE

DRY STONE WALL

LIE-BYE

ENGINE SIDING

1 IN 35 UP

1 IN 35 UP PW

S/BOX

ENGINE SIDING

C ST

LOCOMEN'S MESS

IAIN

SAND

OFFICE

STORE

LOCO SHED

VB

LIFT-OFF SCENERY FOR ACCESS

TARN

BECK

VIADUCT

S/BOX

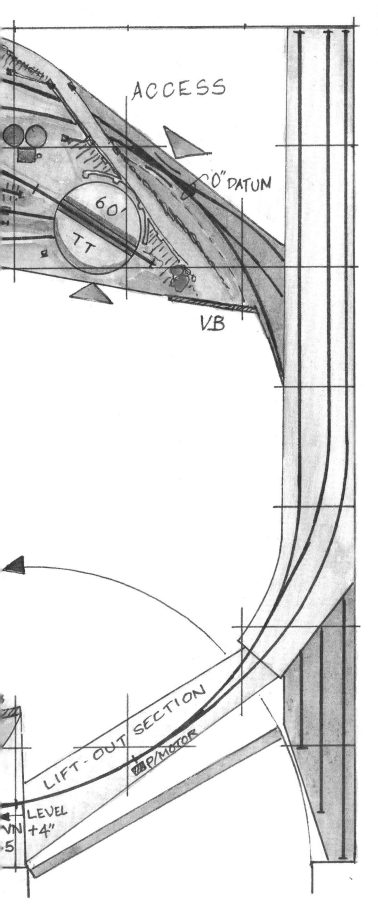

ACCESS

"O" DATUM

60' TT

VB

LIFT - OUT SECTION

P/MOTOR

LEVEL +4"

N +4"

-5

days, six was a good load - most expresses seem to have been four or so handsome Bain bogie clerestory coaches and a six-wheel luggage van behind a class 2 4-4-0 (or two). Compact trains for compact layouts.

The direct inspiration for this design is Rowsley, the point at the southern end of the traverse of the High Peak at which assisting engines were often attached and detached. Rowsley has an odd sort of layout - the original station was the terminus of a branch and when the line was extended further north it was on the wrong alignment, so a new station was built to the south-west of the town. The first station - as 'Rowsley Town' - ended up as a goods depot on the end of a very short stub branch, while its successor handled the main line trains and the extensive locomotive work. There were not one but two loco sheds at Rowsley to handle all the assisting engine requirements and - given the nature of the line, steeply graded (much at 1 in 90) and sharply curved, with some seriously heavy engineering in the matter of bridges and tunnels - most trains needed assistance.

Rowsley would be far too ambitious a subject for a model - certainly, any model intended for a modest space - so Rowtor is a very cut-down 'take' on the same theme of an 'assisting engine station'. On this minimum-space site, I haven't attempted to include the station proper. Centrepiece of the layout is the MPD and the access arrangements for attaching/removing pilot engines, a track layout based on that given in W A Tuplin's 'Midland Steam' and incorporating - in best Midland style - no facing points in a running line.

The MPD includes a classic MR 3-road hipped-roof shed that will hold six typical tender engines, with a 60-foot turntable to turn them and 'all usual facilities' - a big water tank with softening plant (Peak District water is heavy in lime salts) and a 'coal hole'. Water cranes are also sited by the running lines for the use of train engines topping-off their tanks while pilots are attached. Ashpits and boiler washout tracks are also provided, and the whole MPD is conceived very much as a 'showpiece' around which the rest of the layout is arranged.

Nuts and Bolts

This is another variation on the 'end-to-end-up-a-hill' concept, with two fiddleyards stacked one above the other along one short wall. The longest siding each way will take a six-coach train and a 4-6-0. The visible main line is, like the prototpe - double track throughout, although singled in the approaches to the fiddleyards to avoid lots of pointwork. The gradient up from Rowtor is a walloping 1 in 35, which should look steep enough to call for a pilot engine in anybody's book, as well as being needed to achieve a four-inch vertical separation of the fiddleyards - just about the practicable minimum. The way I arrange trackbeds and framing for 'minimum separation' yards like these is shown in the thumbnail sketch.

Double deck fiddleyard.

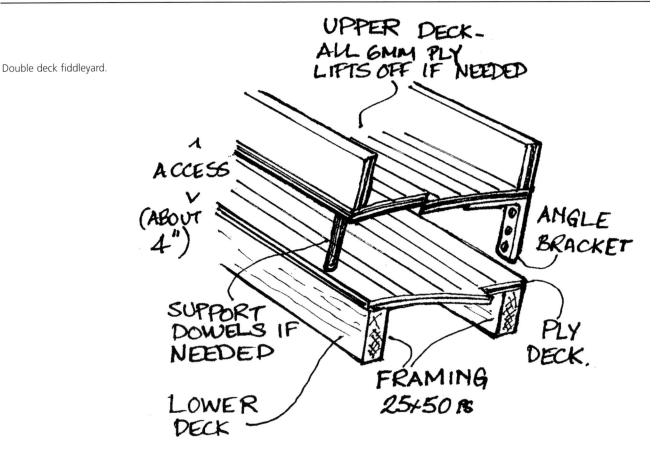

UPPER DECK -
ALL 6MM PLY
LIFTS OFF IF NEEDED

ACCESS
(ABOUT 4")

ANGLE BRACKET

SUPPORT DOWELS IF NEEDED

PLY DECK.

FRAMING 25×50 ß

LOWER DECK

I suppose you could execute this layout in Peco track - with a bit of jiggling to fit around their standard point geometry - but I'd want proper chaired bullhead PW for a pre-group context. SMP with copper-clad pointwork would serve, but it might well be worth going the whole hog and using C & L flex-track with ply-and-rivet pointwork decorated with C & L chairs - a combination that works just as well for fine-scale 00 as it does for more exacting standards. With 2' 9" limiting curves, this is really a 00 layout only on this site; to build it in EM I think you would need to go at least up to the 12 x 8 site size, while P4 would just about be possible on 14 x 9.

If I were building something like this, I'd go for either the later Midland or early LMS periods. As well as the ubiquitous Compound, 4F and 2P, the modern RTR ranges offer such apposite plums as Bachman's magnificent new 'Crab'. Ratio do some nice short (50ft?) MR clerestory coaches although I have a sneaking feeling they're not quite the right ones, and Slater's offer that characteristic and characterful 6-wheel clerestory brake van. For the later LMS/early BR period, Stanier period 1 (panelled) coaches are also available RTR, and there are lots of appropriate locos to choose from: Class 5, Royal Scot, Jubilee, Patriot, 8F, Ivatt 2-6-2T and, of course, the older prototypes already mentioned. As a minimal-space 'craftsmans' layout, this is also a subject with a lot to offer - it would suit a keen loco builder, as the MPD would make a good display area for a varied stud of MR power. For those with a penchant for etched brasss and matters Midland, Alan Gibson has an amazingly wide choice of suitable locomo-

tive types in his range. The examples I've built over the years have all gone together well and made excellent models.

Operationally, this is a 'parade of trains' affair, with the bonus of pilot engines being added or taken off. In the 'up' direction there's also a goods lie-bye siding, which extends 'off scene' beneath the rocky outcroppings of Row Tor itself. The rockwork is made removable for access to this hidden track, and to the main running lines in the tunnel. The viaduct is, of course, inspired by Miller's Dale, and the whole of the 'secondary scene' is simply an excuse for some knock-your-socks off scenic modelling to form a great setting for the trains.

Summary:
Subject: MR/LMS/early BR in Peak District.
Scale/gauge: 4mm/16.5mm finescale 00.
Site size: 10 x 7 feet.
Ruling curve radius: 2ft 9ins.
Ruling grade: 1 in 35.
Longest fiddleyard road: 5ft 10ins.

Further reading:
Midland Steam,
by W A Tuplin. D & C 1973.
Regional History of the Railways of Britain, Vols 9
(East Midlands) and 10 (The North West) D & C/various.
Forgotten Railways - the East Midlands,
by P Howard Anderson. D & C, 1973.

Port Isaac Road
North Cornwall Line

I make no apologies for returning to Cornwall for another design, this time Southern rather than Western, based on the immortal 'Withered Arm' - a lifelong Rice favourite that is now, alas, but a memory. But there was a time - in the late 1950s and early 1960s - when the Rice family repared annually for a summer holiday on a Cornish farm, at St Issey near Padstow. Unlike the previous summer locale - Thrupe Farm, Masbury, right at the summit of the Somerset and Dorset (of which more anon) - Higher Petherick farmhouse didn't offer a railway passing a mere field's-width away; it was a whole three fields, down the hill towards the wonderful wide shimmering estuary of the River Camel, and the last far-flung extremity of Waterloo's push to the west, the Padstow line.

It was on this stretch of railway that I encountered the two extremes of Southern Region motive power: the magnificent, sleek, 'air smoothed' Bullied light pacifics - and the seemingly-immortal, ancient, anachronistic Beattie well-tanks, still kept to toil over the eleven twisting miles up to Wenford Bridge and occasionally 'filling in' on the Padstow turn. How does one choose a favourite from such diversity? Well, being only twelve at the time, I thought the Beatties were jolly, but the Bullieds were awesome. To me, they were the very symbol of power and progress, and even today remain a firm favourite (unrebuilt, of course; rebuilt engines never came down to Cornwall, and anyway were far less distinctive than a 'Spam Can').

The North Cornnwall line of those days offered other delights - although these changed from year to year. Local trains to Padstow or Bodmin were the province of the neat Adams 02 0-4-4Ts, another old friend from Isle of Wight holidays when I was very small, while the last handful of T9s was still working out of Okehampton and would sometimes turn up on the stopping trains. Then there were the N class Moguls - not very exciting, but a comely engine for all that, and they did have Walschaerts valve gear. As did the Ivatt Class 2 2-6-2Ts of LMS origin which replaced the 02s around 1960, and the BR Standard class 4 2-6-4Ts whch saw off the T9s. I even quite liked the ex-GWR 1366 class 0-6-0PT which eventually pensioned off the well tanks.

Very much a lesser main line, but still qualifying. An up express - three whole coaches - on the North Cornwall line.
Author's Collection.

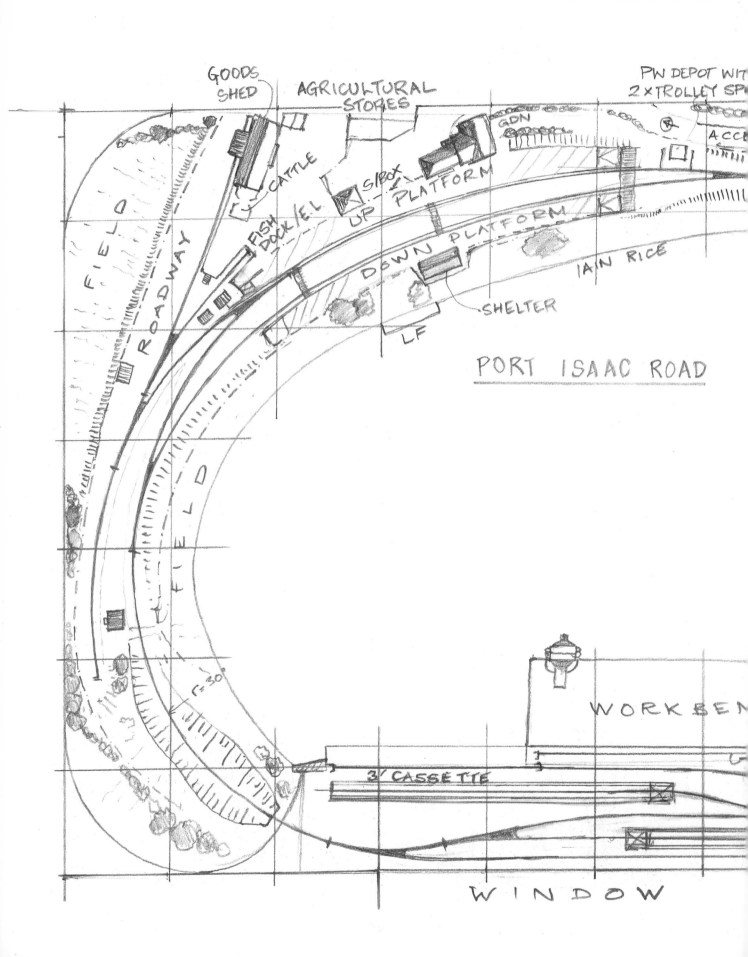

GOODS SHED

AGRICULTURAL STORES

PW DEPOT WITH 2 × TROLLEY SP

ACC

GDN

S/BOX

UP PLATFORM

CATTLE

FISH DOCK/EL

DOWN PLATFORM

IAN RICE

SHELTER

LF

PORT ISAAC ROAD

FIELD

ROADWAY

FIELD

FIELD

r=30"

WORK BEN

3' CASSETTE

WINDOW

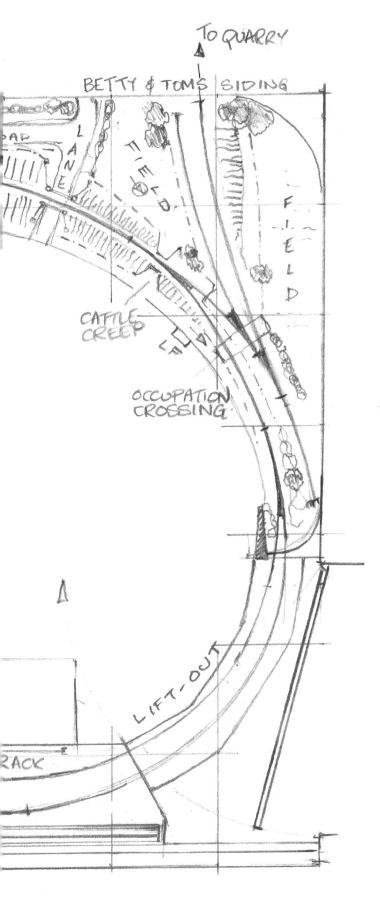

TO QUARRY

BETTY & TOM'S SIDING

CATTLE CREEP

OCCUPATION CROSSING

LIFT-OUT

I don't know how many trips I made over the North Cornwall line between 1959 and 1964, but I do remember that it was always an event. The excitement really started at Meldon, when the train reeled out over that spindly viaduct, then swung right at Fatherford Junction towards the gorse-blazened heights of Maddaford Moor on a curve so tight you could see the engine easily from about the third coach back. Halwill Junction was always a mystery - it had all the appearance of being an important station, but there was no town! Launceston, on the other hand, was not just a fascinating 'double station', but a town of the most romantic and satisfactory sort, crowned by its castle. It was also the entrance to Cornwall and hence the gateway to a magic land, where stations had strange names like Egloskerry and Tresmeer, wild and widswept Otterham, Camelford, Delabole, Port Isaac Road and St Kew Highway.

Of course, being young and impressionable, when it came to train-watching I gave the North Cornwall 'main line' the cold shoulder (not enough trains) and set off for the GWR and Bodmin Road. I'm ashamed to say I usually took the bus, as it was quicker and cheaper than going by train, but in later, bicycling years I'd follow the B & W line up the Camel Valley to Dunmere before skirting around the town of Bodmin (which, like Launceston, sits on top of a hill) on the back-lanes and cutting across to Bodmin Road station on the GWR main line. If I only had an afternoon, then Wadebridge itself was a very acceptable substitute; there was usually a well-tank scuttling around on pilot duties, while another would appear in mid-afternoon with the goods from Wenford. The arrival of the Atlantic Coast Express at tea-time made a pleasing finale to the day.

Port Isaac Road - a suitable case for treatment
In selecting a North Cornwall line subject for the basis of a minimal-space layout design, I have adhered to the 'smaller station' theme. Port Isaac Road and St Kew Highway are very similar in general situation and layout, both conveniently being curved and both 'up high'. What swung the decision in favour of Port Isaac Road is its slightly more compact goods yard - important in a minimum-space essay like this - and the proximity of two further useful Layout design elements - Trelill Tunnel (the only one on the line, oddly enough) to the south and Betty & Toms's quarry to the north - with a gated siding and spur. Of course, all this is hopelessly compressed to get it into 10 x 7 feet, but there are no fundamental compromises and the overall track layout is true to prototype even if the loop is miles too short - there is just room for a four-coach train to pass opposing traffic. Conveniently, four coaches (or rather, three coaches and a bogie 'B' van for newspaper and perishables traffic) was the usual 'maximum formation' for regular North Cornwall Line trains.

The other classic North Cornwall signature locomotive - the ex-LSW 'T9' 4-4-0. 30715 is on the turntable at Padstow, farthest-flung outpost of the Southern Region. *Author's Collection.*

This is basically a 00 gauge design, as the 2' 6" ruling curve is just a tad tight for EM and impossible for P4. But it's OK in 16.5mm gauge, even with Bullied light pacifics (which were in reality amazingly forgiving engines on sharply-curved track). This layout would be definitely buildable in fine scale if one went up to the next size of site, the 12 x 8 garden shed. The fiddleyard is an example of the 'double stub off a continuous-run' - effectively a single-ended 2-road fiddle-yard for each direction to allow for end-to-end working, with a link section for continuous running. Each fiddleyard has a single long road, capable of holding a six-coach 'Altlantic Coast Express' and light pacific; the second fiddleyard road in each of the the yards leads on to a much shorter (3 ft.) cassette, used to handle local passenger and freight workings. These cassettes are interchangeable, and spare units could stored on shelf track on the wall either side of the window.

Again, this is a relatively simple layout that could be built with Peco track (code 75, please) although scale bullhead (SMP or C & L) would look better. Obviously, there isn't huge operational scope, but you should be able to replicate just about any prototype working up to and including the 'ACE' to scale length. Several appropriate locos are available in modern high-quality RTR: Bachmann have the SR 'N' Mogul, the BR Standard 4 2-6-4T and the Ivatt 2-6-2T, while Hornby can provide you with an excellent light pacific. The T9 and 02 are both available in cast whitemetal (Westward, SE Finecast) or etched-brass (Finney, Gibson) kit form should you fancy the slightly earlier period.

Coaching stock is very slightly more problematic. Bachmann do a nice scale-length Bullied coach and superb BR Mk1s, either of which will serve for the 'ACE'. These types were not standard fare on the general North Cornwall line workings, however, where the older Maunsell type held sway. The old Ian Kirk plastic Maunsell coach kits are still available from Colin Ashby and make quite a reasonable model with a bit of work. Roxey do etched versions, although, like the Kirk kits, these lack the outside window-retaining mouldings that are such a characteristic of these coaches. A modern-standard RTR Maunsell would be nice, very nice.....

Summary:

Subject: BR (SR) C1960, North Cornwall.

Scale/gauge: 4mm/16.5mm fine 00.

Site size: 10 x 7 feet.

Ruling curve radius: 2ft 6ins (hidden).

Ruling grade: none.

Longest fiddleyard road: 6ft.

Further reading:

An Illustrated History of the North Cornwall Railway,
by David Wroe. Irwell, 1994.
The Withered Arm,
by T W E Roche, Town & Country Press, 1967.
The Sothern Railway's Withered Arm - A View from the past,
by Stephen Austin. Ian Allan, 1998.

Melling
Kent

That's right, it's Melling with an e not Malling with an a. Which means that it doesn't exist, unlike the latter, which is a mile or two on the Sevenoaks side of Maidstone. Imaginary Melling, on the other hand, is deemed to be deep in the heart of rural Kent, on the ex-LCDR route from Maidstone to Ashford - a setting straight out of the pages of an H E Bates short story. This is a rolling landscape of gentle valleys, hanging woodlands, orchards and hop-gardens, dene-holes and dew-ponds. A lanscape dotted with fine old farmhouses and cottages in soft Kentish brick and white weatherboarding, under undulating roofs of rich red tiles, with the distictive pyramids or cones of the hop-oasts peeking from amid sweeping stands of elm. In other words, this is a very beautiful and very modellable setting through which to run some very beautiful and modellable trains.

The SE & CR in high Kent is like a box of especially delicious chocolates; one doesn't know where to start, which of the many delights should be sampled first. Leaving aside the lusciousness of the landscape for a moment, just consider the virtues of the trains as grist to the modelling mill: Firstly, there's that livery. Why the SE & CR (both constituents of which had for years applied austere black paint schemes to their locomotives) selected one of the most hedonistic of all pre-group liveries, a wonderful deep wine-bottle green set off by a plethora of lining, polished brass and rich chocolate lake framing, is something of a mystery. But they did, a fact we can only be thankful

Main line trains don't come much more modellagenic than this - an 'LT' and 4-5 'Birdcage' coaches. *Author's Collection.*

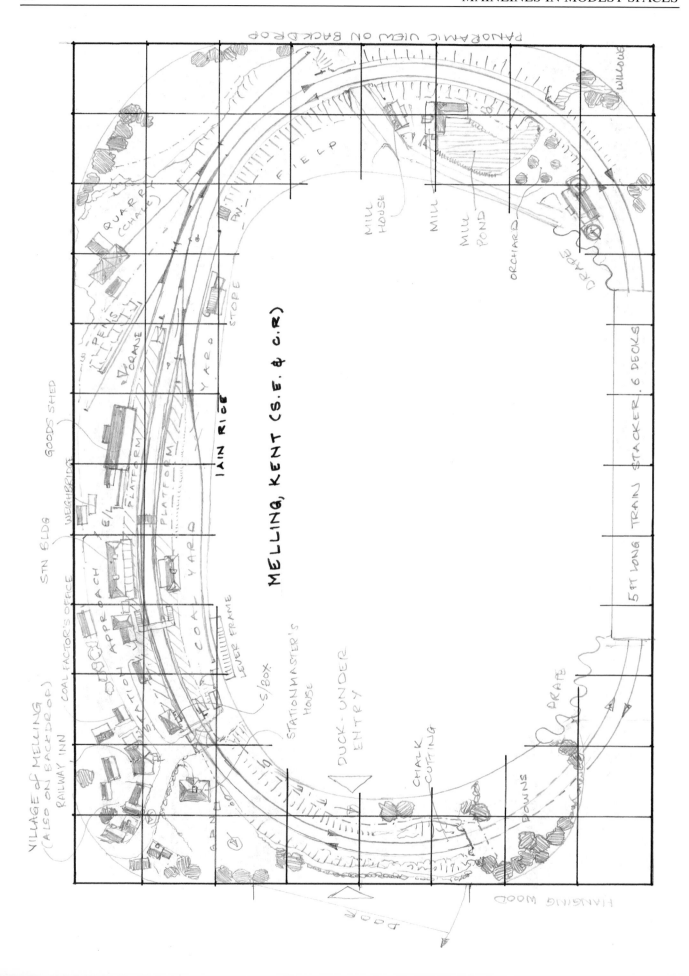

MELLING, KENT (S.E. & C.R)

IAIN RICE

ABOVE: An SECR secondary express headed by engine 676 - SECR class G - the first of five engines of Great North of Scotland Railway design bought in 1900 to alleviate a motive power crisis. Seen with the usual very mixed rake of bogies and six-wheel stock and running on typical ballasted-all-over SER permanent way. *Author's Collection.*

RIGHT: The SECR is not generally thought of as a freight line, but they did in fact have a considerable goods traffic, including considerable quantities of bunker coal for the various cross-channel steamers. This looks like a coal train, toiling out of London behind two handsome SER Stirling 'O' series goods engines. *Author's Collection.*

for. Well-executed on a model, the SE & C livery is equalled probably only by the Brighton, Furness, Caley and M & GN.

And then there are the locomotives to which this gorgeous decoration was applied. Harry S Wainwright is widely regarded as the doyen of locomotive designers of his day, the equal of S W Johnson, J G Robinson or Dugald Drummond when it came to happy proportions and purity of line. The immortal D class 4-4-0s, the stalwart C class goods and the sprightly H classs 0-4-4Ts were not only highly successful

locomotives in the practical sense, but rank among the most beautiful designs ever to run in this country. Not that the Chatham's contribution was lacking in looks; the Kirtley 4-4-0s of the 'M' series were outstandingly handsome locomotives, while the same designer's B series 0-6-0s were a very comely example of the type, to which the Wainwright 'C' bears a more-than-passing resemblance.

And if that is not a great enough largesse, we then have some of the finest coaching stock built in the grand tradition

Secondary passenger workings could also be 'interesting'; here, five ancient four wheel coaches - including two with 'birdcage' look-outs - and a six-wheeler are trailing a trio of cattle vans, all behind a smart new Wainwright 'H' class 0-4-4T. *Author's Collection.*

of Victorian panelled construction, but with an Edwardian restraint, elegance of line and finesse of detail, finished in a wonderful rich ruby lake - the colour of a glass of exceptionally good port. That these coaches are not over-long, are simple of outline (and consequently not too difficult to model from a very good choice of etched kits) only adds to the appeal. Even the finishing isn't too hard, as the lake paint was unadorned by lining; it didn't need to be - there was enough elaboration on an SE & C loco to make do for the whole train...

Modelling the SE & C

As a modelling proposition, the SE & CR in its early years (1899 - 1914) has an awful lot going for it. (It's not at all bad later on, but you have to pass on the peachy paint scheme in favour of unlined battleship grey.) As a main line subject for a modest space, it's right with the Midland or the GC as an eminently attainable prototype. For a start, there are some truly excellent kits out there for SE & C engines - the Wills (now SE Finecast) range includes the three Wainwright classics as well as the diminutive P class, the later 'E' 4-4-0, the 'S' class 0-6-0ST (a C with a hat on) and the ex-Chatham Kirtley 'R1' 0-4-4T - not to mention a dinky little crane tank - while the Horby-Dublo R1 0-6-0T was the first passably accurate plastic-bodied RTR locomotive. That little lot would give you a pretty sound basis for any 1900 - 1914 SE & C layout, without considering such esoterica as Falcon Brass' Stirling 01 0-6-0, F and B class 4-4-0s and 'Q' 0-4-4T. For the later period, DJH do an 'L' class 4-4-0 and SE Finecast the 'River' and 'W' classes of 2-6-4T - while Bachmann, of course, will sell you a first-class RTR model of Mr Maunsell's magnificent mogul. Years ago, Tri-ang(modern Hornby) also produced a version

of the L1 (reboiled 'L') 4-4-0 that was not half bad and, with a bit of work, made a pretty fair model. For a 'not very popular' prototype the SE & C is actually very well served!

It's the same story with the coaching stock, with not just the newer and better-known 'Birdcage' stock (Blacksmith) out there, but a pretty good selection of older types including 4 and 6-wheel stock of both the consituent companies in the excellent 'Roxey' range. The only area a bit lacking is freight stock, but it's to be had from the likes of Chivers Finelines. The ubiquitous SR box van (Ratio/Bachmann), round-end open (ABS) and 25-ton brake van (Cambrian) were essentially SECR designs, as, of course, were the famous 'utility vans' (Parkside, Ratio, Uncle Tom Cobley and all). The HMRS rub-down/Methfix range includes a variety of SECR transfers. Only the earlier goods vehicles are difficult to come by - but then, what else was Plastikard invented for?

As for the layout design itself, then there's not a huge amount to say as it's pretty conventional fare - a simple and modest wayside station with a basic oval format on a 12 x 8 garden shed site. The only exception to convention is the inclusion of a 'train stacker' vertically sliding fiddle yard. But this could be replaced by normal cassettes or, where a bit more width was available, by a traverser. The Layout Design Elements are all Kentish classics (or clichés, if you're being unkind), including a chalk cutting, a weatherboarded mill beside a placid stream, an agricultural group with Kentish barn and oast, an orchard and a typically oddball set of LCD station buildings. (LCD stations were often oddball because they were built piecemeal and on the cheap, the company being perpetually on the brink of Chancery). Other signature items are the Chatham signals with their distinctive 6-foot

A boat train on the old South Eastern main line through Tonbridge, behind a Stirling 'F' class 4-4-0. Note the complex head code, typical of the SER and SECR lines in Kent. *Oilette Postcard/Author's Collection.*

arms and the 'ballasted all over except for every sixth sleeper' PW. At the far end of the shed, facing you as you come in, the line is deemed to run on an embankment above high ground, with a panoramic vista over the Weald presented on the backdrop - what the Americans would call a 'Greet Scene'

Really, this scheme is all about the joys of modelling such an intimate and detailed landscape (Barry Norman's book to the fore, with interjections from Tony Hill and Gordon Gravett) and, of course, the multi-chromic maze of the loco livery - which actually isn't as bad as some would have you believe, especially in these days of transfer film and acrylic lining inks that go through Rotring pens. I've envisaged this principally as an EM or P4 layout, as it's aimed more at the kitbuilder than the RTR buyer. Apart from other considerations, the ruling 3ft 0ins transitioned curves are designed to suit smaller locomotives in fine scale - but there's no reason why a more 'up to date' version featuring 'Schools' and Bullied pacifics shouldn't be executed on modern 00.

All the layouts I present in these books represent projects that I would be happy to try myself (keep taking the pills, Iain; life begins at 55) - but if ever I get 12 x 8 unobstructed feet for a layout, this one's near the top of my list. I even have the C class and the R1 to get me started...

This is a layout design dedicated to the memory of my old friend Martin Brent, who did so much to introduce me (and many others) to the delights of Kent and its railways. His 'Hope Mill' layout formed a large part of the inspiration for Melling... spot the similarities! Sorely missed, is Martin.

Summary:

Subject: SECR/SR/BR(S) secondary main line in Kent c1910, or later.

Scale/gauge: 4mm: P4/EM/fine 00.

Site size: 12 x 8ft garden shed.

Ruling curve radius: 36".

Ruling grade: none.

Longest fiddleyard road: 63".

Further Reading:

New Century on the South Eastern & Chatham Railway, by John Minnis. WSP 1985.

The South Eastern and Chatham Railway, by O S Nock. Ian Allan, 1961.

Boat Trains & Chennel Packets, by Rixon Bucknall. Stuart, 1957.

The South Eastern & Chatham Railway, by R W Kidner. Oakwood Press, 1963.

Douneblane

If ever a steam locomotive looked as if it was built purely for speed and nothing else, that engine has to be the Gresley A4 pacific. It was to most of its contemporaries what a Bugatti 'Atlantic' coupé was to an Austin 16; exotic, almost unworldly, and quite, quite beautiful. That it was fast - the very the fastest such machine, then or since - went almost without saying. Indeed, it was ultimately faster (by a few miles an hour) even than the beguiling Bugatti, for all the racing heritage that lay beneath that svelte streamlined shell. The A4 was every inch a thoroughbred, 'pur sang', the ultimate and unalloyed expression of the very concept of an 'express' locomotive.

To the fortunate and youthful Rice, the A4s were familiar things - the object of many a trip to the lineside of the old Great Northern raceway down to London. An A4 on the GN was a crescendo that started with a long tenor note in the distance and built rapidly to a throbbing three-cylinder purr beneath the menacing staccato of that Kylchap double blastpipe, a flash of tall wheels and whirling motion, gleaming green paint reflecting the sun in a long, low arc off the boiler casing. And in an instant - past, as fast as you could turn your head, hunched and purposeful when seen from astern, the exhaust steam drifting down over your head as the urgent beat of the Gresley bogies bounding over the rail joints gave way to a rapidly-dwindling tail light. There was no other sight like it.

Imagine my horror when in 1964 - by which time Potters Bar, Hadley Wood and Hatfield were utterly devoid of chime whistles and Kylchap exhausts, and the best that might be hoped for was a thundering 'Deltic' in full cry - I next met an A4. It was at Galashiels station, on the dying Waverley route, during a dour Scottish spring holiday when, I recall, it rained every single day. As I came onto the platform in the hope of some trains to inspire me, there on the 'up' road - dimmed only by the drizzle - was that unmistakable outline. But unbelievably - filthy dirty, leaking steam, dented and dishevelled, and at the head of a lowly pick-up goods train. 'Andrew K McCosh' had come down a long, long way in the world - quite literally, it was the sight of a thoroughbred pulling a coal cart. I turned around and walked straight back off the platform. How could anyone do such a thing to so magical and magnificent a machine? That was the last time I ever saw an A4 in British Railways service, but it is not how I want to remember them. It was a sour tasting aftermath.

Elsewhere in Scotland, however, did I but know it, I could have seen A4s in far happier circumstances, living out one last glorious swansong of streamlined steam on the old Caledonian route northward through Perth to Aberdeen, on the legendary 'Three Hour' expresses from Glasgow and Edinburgh. On tracks where the immortal Caledonian 123 (truly a 'Bugatti' locomotive of an earlier age) had once streaked northwards in the race to beat the North British to Kinnaber Junction and hence on to Aberdeen, the LNER pacifics - A4s, some A3s, and the Peppercorn A2s - now held sway, and that three hour schedule could be bettered by a quarter of an hour if need be.

So it would still have been possible, in 1964 and for a brief while thereafter, to relish once more the sight of an A4 in full cry, racing over the level stretches north of Stirling before the first stern test, the climb up to the bleak summit on the Ochill moors between Blackford and Geneagles, then charging off again down the long straight descent through Auchterarder and onward to Hilton Junction, deep in its rocky defile through the Montcrieff Hill that defended Perth from the south. I never knew this line at first hand, but I've heard tales of it from those that did, and enjoyed Derek Cross's wonderful pictures of the Gresley engines on those Aberdeen trains. (Trains of usually no more than eight or nine coaches, moreover, made for modelling in modest spaces!).

Of Doune and Allan Waters

Dunblane is a place notorious in modern times for one of the most dreadful and incomprehensible of tragedies. But in happier times it was known as a genteel city of the best provincial Scottish sort, elegant and serene, lying dignified on a gentle hillside crowned with a squat, solid, square-towered cathedral church. Dunblane - in railway terms - is a classic junction, where the Dunblane and Callander railway swings away to the west while the main line sets its cap at the pass of the Allan Water between the heights of Glenartney Forest on the one hand and the Ochill Hills on the other. The Dunblane and

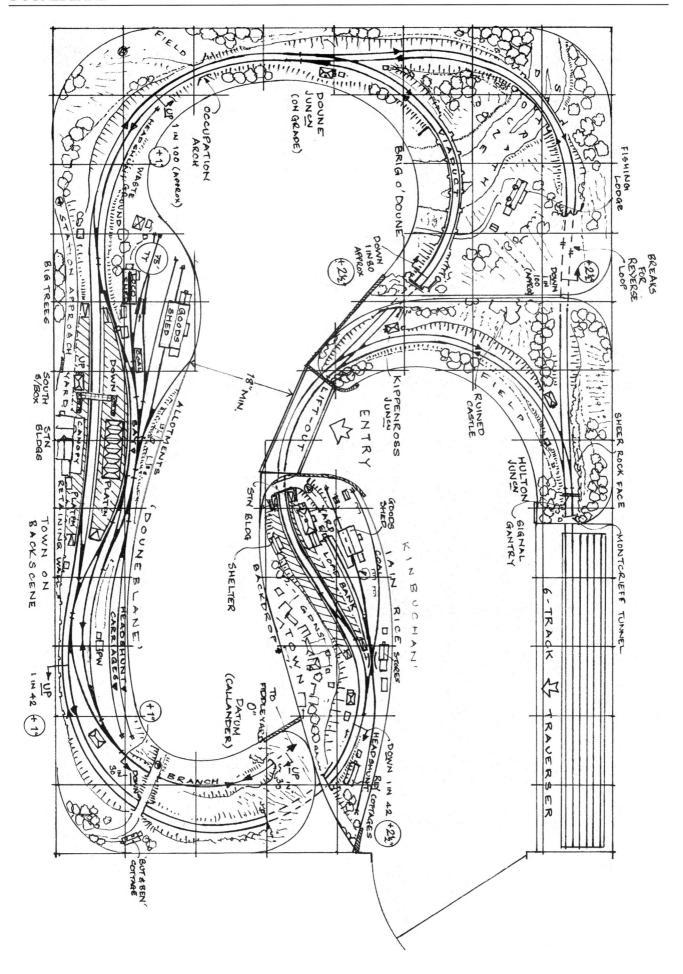

Callander was, of course, the stump onto which was eventually grafted the long, long trailing branch of the Callander and Oban, which finished up facing the Western Isles on the other side of Scotland altogether.

So Dunblane, as a compact junction with an attractive setting, a good range of typical Caledonian buildings and some very compelling trains, struck me as a good centrepiece for a fairly ambitious N scale layout based on the ex-Caledonian main line between Stirling and Perth as it was circa 1964. As well as the junction station 'Douneblane', the layout includes a scene based on Hilton Junction at Perth (Hulton Junction on the model), a secondary wayside station (Kinbuchan) and some rather clichéd Scottish scenic elements. I've changed the spelling of the place names somewhat as I've taken more than a few liberties with the prototypes, although 'Douneblane' is quite closely based on Dunblane in general layout and Hulton Junction is Hilton in all but name. Kinbuchan, however, bears little if any resemblance to the real Kinbuck, while Kippenross Junction is an utter fiction, as is Doune. 'Brig o'Doune' is an appalling pun fit to turn any Scotsman in his grave, while the whole of Strath Doune à la Rice is as unreal as Never-Never Land. It's just an excuse for a couple of nice bridges and a model of a white-painted fishing lodge.

Essentially, this is a 'teardrop' layout arranged as a series of discreet scenes, featuring a reverse-loop double-track main line running out and back from the 6-road traverser fiddleyard, with a link added to permit continuous running. The fiddleyard is effectively 'Perth', which in reality lies immediately beyond the Montcrieff Tunnel. Trains leaving the tunnel can either swing left on to 'North British' metals or carry straight on over the Caley. On the layout, if they turn left then they're going 'south' via Kippenross and Kinbuchan to enter Douneblane from the north (quite an achievement, given that

somewhere between Hulton and Kinbuchan the NBR to Dunfermline and the Forth Bridge has become the CR north of Kinbuck!). Heading 'north' via Doune Junction, the trains descend a long gentle grade to enter Douneblane from the south on a wide curve - a real 'racing stretch' on which to let an N scale A4 have its head. 'North' of Douneblane, the line starts climb in earnest - 1 in 42 - to reach Kinbuchan.

The branch line to Callander also leaves the north end of Douneblane but on an unprototypical falling grade of no less than 1 in 30 - the objective being to get sufficient vertical clearance for a 'Callander' fiddleyard to be sited beneath Kinbuchan. The grades shown give 2½" headroom - tight, but not impossible. Steepening them could release more headroom, but all that is needed here is a very simple cassette or sector table for the branch train. The Callander line was on its last legs in 1964 - a landslide in Glen Ogle the following autumn severed the route between Callander and Crianlarich, and the truncated remains eastward to Dunblane died barely a month later, closed on 31st October 1965. The steam trains soon followed the branch into oblivion.

The section from Doune Junction to Kippenross is, of course, merely the link necessary to complete a continuous run, for those occasions when a little simple lappery is all that is required of the layout. The necessary electrical breaks in the 'reverse loop' section between Doune Junction and Hulton Junction - where polarity needs reversing for the train to continue in the correct direction on conventional control - are sited in the 'dead area' of the tunnel. The best way of avoiding a glitch as the train traverses this point is to use separate sections with matching controllers either side of the break, so that the correct polarities can be set up before the train arrives and progress will be all-but seamless. Using a

In an earlier period, the other great streamlined Gresley design also worked through to Aberdeen. Here is LNER 2002 'Earl Marischall' leaving Aberdeen 1.40 express fish to London via Edinburgh. This train was a crack working and often rated an A4 further south.
C. Lawson Ken/Author's Collection.

The Gresley A4 pacific, the Bugatti of the railway world. These engines had their swansong on the old Caley route to Aberdeen via Dunblane.
Author's Collection.

DCC system would, of course, avoid the problem altogether; on a layout of this type - which could be operated almost entirely with tender locos or diesels allowing the fitting of decoders - this is quite possible.

Although conceived as a showcase for the last years of steam, this layout could easily be moved forward into the diesel era - the staple traction to replace the pacifics being the ubiquitous class 47, in the original green scheme from 1966 - mid 1970s, then dull old blue, and subsequently ScotRail's variant of the Intercity livery; Intercity HST sets took over in the early 1990s. Other classes to see out steam on this Caley route included the Stanier class 5 and various BR types - including some of the 'Clans' and the odd 'Britannia', the standard 5 4-6-0s and the handsome class 4 2-6-4Ts. Early diesel traction to feature alongside the steamers included theD80XX series Bo-Bos (TOPs class 20) and the ill-fated D61XX North British diesel-hydraulics - which barely survived long enough to be TOPed at all. 3-car Derby DMUs of class 107 took over the stopping trains, succeeded in the later diesel era by 'Super Sprinters'. I expect it's all 156 turbos today. Whatever the chosen era, a good selection of the requisite locomotive types are available in modern N scale RTR, as are the accompanying BR Mk1 and Mk2 coaches.

But really, the objective of this scheme is to be able to enjoy once again the sight of those unique Gresley streamliners racing through a handsome landscape, living out to the last the purpose for which they were designed: express passenger working.

Summary:
Subject: Ex-CR main line between Stirling and Perth, 1964.
Scale/gauge: N scale.
Site size: 12 x 8 shed.
Ruling curve radius: 21" (on continuous link). Most curves 24".
Ruling grade: 1 in 42 (main) 1 in 30 (branch).
Longest fiddleyard road: 4ft 6ins.

Further reading:
British Railways Past and Present No 9 - South and East Scotland, by Keith Sanders & Douglas Hodgins. Silver Link, 1991.
The Caledonian Railway, by O S Nock. Ian Allan, 1963.
The Callander and Oban railway, by John Thomas. D & C, 1966.
The Gresley Pacifics, Vol 2.
O S Nock, D & C 1975.
Scottish Railways in the Heyday of Steam, by H C Casserley. Bradford Barton, undated.

Milton Junction
NER/Newcastle & Carlisle Section

Cross-country railways: A catch-all category for lines - of extremely varied character - that join two or more important locations, but without serving anywhere much of note in between, and which don't go to London. Cross-country lines can be anything from the meandering single-track weight-restricted byways of East Anglia or Mid-Wales to busy double-tracked routes used by the heaviest trains. Somewhere in between these extremes (but, I'd suggest, closer to the heavy main line end) comes the inspiration for this little essay, the Newcastle & Carlisle.

Newcastle is the centre of a huge, sprawling conurbation, one of the powerhouses of British heavy industry. Carlisle is an important provincial city, a border point, citadel, and major centre of industry, trade and transport - in the modern parlance, a 'regional hub'. Carlisle Citadel in its heyday was one of the largest and busiest railway junctions in Britain, a classic 'Joint' station and one - served, in pre-group days - by more railway companies than any other single location. Even today, Carlisle is a major player in the transportation business - not least as home to one of Europe's largest and most successful road hauliers, the eponymous Eddie Stobart.

(As an aside, it's interesting to note how many of the elements that have contributed to the Stobart success story have an echo of railway tradition about them: a smart but dignified livery maintained to a high standard of cleanliness, the naming of individual vehicles, uniformed drivers who have charge of their own 'locos', and a railway-like comprehensiveness to the infrastructure and operating pattern; perhaps we should ask Eddie to go a step further and take on Stobart Rail as well?)

However you choose to view the Newcastle and Carlisle, it was certainly a railway of substantial character. Although it traversed some of the bleakest and most sparsely-populated areas of Britain, it was conceived with double track throughout and engineered on the grand scale common to many early railways (the N & C originated in 1829 and was opened in stages between 1834 and 1838), with relatively easy grades throughout. Laying out such an easy line over such difficult country entailed some heavy engineering works. Although a classic 'river gap' route with a summit level below 500ft, the line featured some massive earthworks (the cutting at Cowran Hills is a mile long and up to 110ft. deep, while an embankment at Hell Beck towered to 73ft) and numerous structures including several viaducts and a major bridge over the Tyne at West Wylam.

The Newcastle and Carlisle certainly viewed itself as a main line, and the very heavy traffic carried - especially in the earlier years - fully justified this status. The line spawned several offshoots - notably, the Alston and Allendale branches and the connection at Hexham with the NBR's straggling Border Counties system. This truly was a 'cross country' line, one that stretched over the Scottish border to remote Riccarton Junction on the Waverley Route, and meandered along by Hadrian's Wall through Morpeth to meet the East Coast Main Line. The N & C also sprouted a tangle of lines serving the mining and manufacturing areas of the lower Tyne Valley. Among these was Wylam, birthplace of George Stephenson and, arguably, of the steam railway concept itself.

Given the nature of the territory crossed by the Newcastle and Carlisle between Naworth in the west and Hexham in the east, it is not surprising to learn that the main traffic was generated at either end of the route - with the North-East's heavy concentration of mining and industry at the eastern end, and the Cumbrian iron fields and the extensive network of collieries and quarries on Lord Carlisle's estates at the west. No wonder then that the line

OPPOSITE PAGE –

TOP: The NER was a very distinctive pre-grouping railway well-served by the specialist trade in 4mm scale. This is a 'Tennant' class 2-4-0, express passsenger power on the Newcastle & Carlisle in the early years of the twentieth century. *Author's Collection.*

LOWER: Mineral traffic on the NER was initially handled by the 'long boiler' type of 0-6-0 that went back to Robert Stephenson and the earliest days of railways. These tough old engines survived into the twentieth century. *Author's Collection.*

attracted the attention of the mighty North Eastern Railway; after a protracted courtship, the two were united in 1862. In later years, the N & C also became a valuable connecting link between the west and east coast main lines, allowing Anglo-Scottish traffic to be diverted across the 'neck of England' should either route be blocked. So, as a prototype for an interesting layout of main line character, the N & C has a lot going for it.

The N & C in miniature

One of the drawbacks of modelling railways like the N & C that are situated in the wide open spaces is that they tend to sprawl somewhat. At the eastern end of the line - certainly as far west as Haltwhistle - many of the stations had staggered platforms, not a very useful arrangement as a basis for a model where space is restricted. At Haltwhistle, the junction

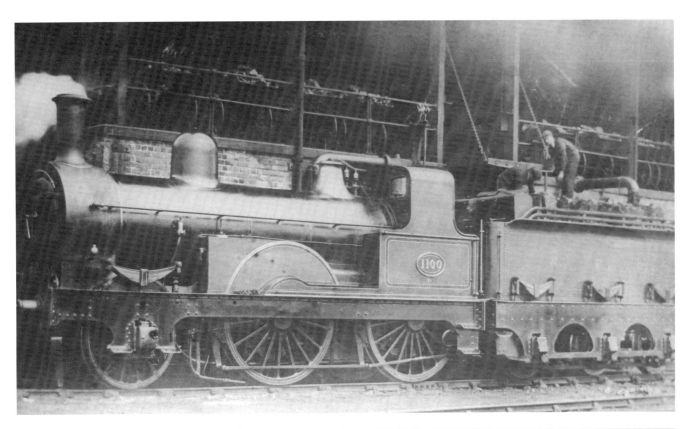

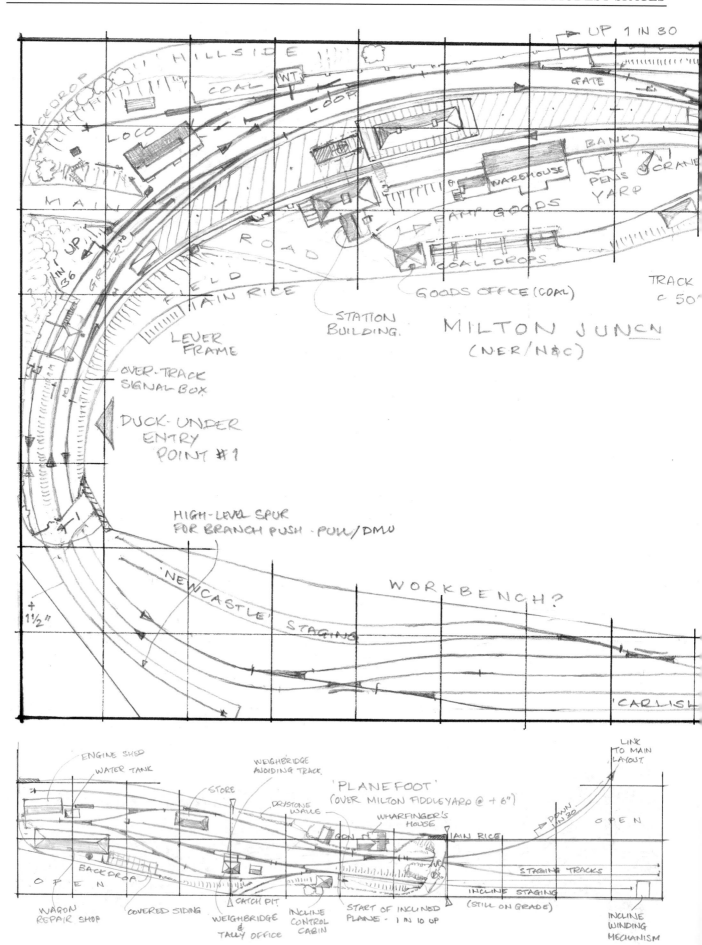

UP 1 IN 30

HILLSIDE

COAL LOOP WT GATE

BACKDROP

LOCO

BANK

WAREHOUSE PENS CRANE YARD

MAIN

UP 1 IN 36 GROUND

ROAD RAMP GOODS

FIELD MAIN RICE COAL DROPS

STATION BUILDING. GOODS OFFICE (COAL) TRACK c 50

LEVER FRAME MILTON JUNCN
(NER/N&C)

OVER-TRACK
SIGNAL BOX

DUCK-UNDER
ENTRY
POINT #1

HIGH-LEVEL SPUR
FOR BRANCH PUSH-PULL/DMU

'NEWCASTLE' STAGING WORKBENCH?

+1½"

'CARLISL

ENGINE SHED WEIGHBRIDGE LINK TO MAIN LAYOUT
WATER TANK AVOIDING TRACK 'PLANEFOOT'
STORE (OVER MILTON FIDDLEYARD @ +6")
DRYSTONE WALLS WHARFINGER'S HOUSE DOWN 1 IN 30 OPEN
GON MAIN RICE
BACKDROP STAGING TRACKS
OPEN INCLINE STAGING
WAGON COVERED SIDING CATCH PIT INCLINE START OF INCLINED (STILL ON GRADE) INCLINE
REPAIR SHOP WEIGHBRIDGE CONTROL PLANE - 1 IN 10 UP WINDING
& TALLY OFFICE CABIN MECHANISM

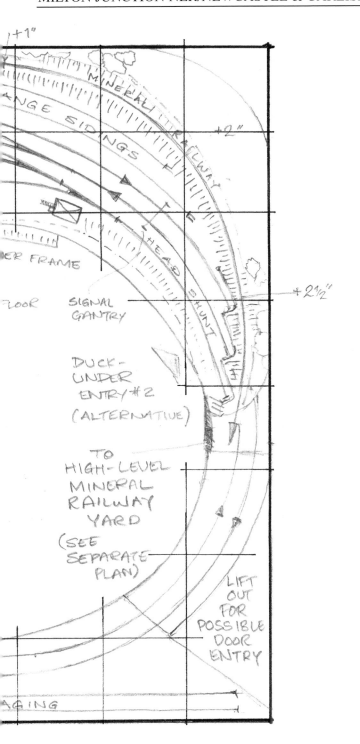

only a very short spur, to Brampton Town. This is somewhat misleading, however, for it was also the junction point with Lord Carlisle's extensive private railway system, the Brampton Railway - a truly fascinating network of early colliery and mineral lines dating back (as a 'waggonway') to 1798. Among other distinctions, Lord Carlisle's Railway owned for a period possibly the most famous steam locomotive of all time - none other than George Stephenson's 'Rocket', sold out of service by the Liverpool & Manchester in 1836. The Brampton Railway finished up as part of the National Coal Board network and ran into the 1950s as such.

The genesis of this (entirely fictional) layout proposal is a combination of the Brampton Junction situation with the island platform layout, to create something that has a decidedly 'North Eastern' feel with a Cumberland/ Durham border setting. The name - Milton - is that by which Brampton Junction was originally known when the N & C first opened. The period I initially had in mind was the early BR era - which permits a very broad mix of locos on the 'main line', up to and including Gresley pacifics (Waverley route engines shedded at Carlisle on 'filling in' turns), although V2s, K3s, Hunt/Shire 4-4-0s and B1s were more typical performers. Also to be seen were many ex-NER survivors such as the hefty R class 4-4-0s (LNER/BR D29), 'P' 0-6-0s (J27) and 'T' class 0-8-0s (Q5/6). BR standard types also appeared, most notably the class 3 and 4 2-6-0s. Main line diesels used included the English Electric 1-Co-Co-1 type 4 (D200 series, TOPS class 40), the Brush Type 4 (D1500/TOPS class 47) and the English Electric type 3 (D67/TOPS Class 37). All of the diesels and most of the LNER/BR steam engines are available RTR.

However, on a slightly more ambitious note, this would make a great pre-grouping layout, the NER being one of those railways that 'models well'. Apart from its innate attractions, the line is well-served by kitmakers: London Road Models, Nu-Cast, Steve Barnfield, Dave Bradwell and DJH all offer NER locos while Slater's, D & S and 51L/David Geen (among others) produce stock. I have included a goodly selection of NER 'signatures' in this scheme - most of which would have lasted into the BR period; the NER built for eternity. So things like the over-track signal cabin, plethora of gantry and bracket signals, coal cells and the substantial Gritstone buildings would probably have lasted into the 1950s.

The N & C fulfils one of my desiderata for a modest main-line layout in its short passenger trains. With a run of only 61 miles from end-to-end, restaurant car facilities were rarely needed and most trains were no more than 4 - 5 carriages. And 4 - 5 carriages behind a V2 or B1 strikes me as a pretty manageable sort of main line train. Diesels arrived from 1958 - on, with many passenger workings being inevitably reduced to DMUs. Other traffics at this period include minerals - iron ore, limestone flux for steelworking and

for the Alston branch, one of the platforms was a broad island, with one straight and one curved face - another very characteristic arrangement associated with the old NER. This is far more adaptable for modelling purposes, as demonstrated by John Wright's beautiful NER 'Benfieldside' EM layout a few years ago.

At the western end of the N & C, where it drops down off of the Pennines toward the Cumbrian coastal plain, there is another junction (Brampton) which - on the face of it - serves

Successors to the long-boiler engines were the Worsdell 0-6-0s, the smaller - and larger-wheeled versions of which were regular
N & C locos - for both of which there is a very good kit in 4mm scale (by London Road Models). *Author's Collection*

power station coal to Blaydon - heavy express goods and parcels traffic, and block tank-wagon trains to convey oil fuel. In the earlier LNER/NER period, you could add livestock and agricultural produce plus engineering goods including substantial items like marine engines, propellers and large castings. Plenty to be going on with.

In addition to the 'main line' part of the layout and the end of the short branch up to the 'town' (a natural for push-pull working, and hence represented on the model by a simple stub staging road) there's also a steeply-graded and tortuously curved mineral line that climbs up and over the main lines to a high-level mineral yard, inspired by Kirkhouse on the Brampton System. This is conceived as a compact, removable and portable affair that could serve as a separate exhibition piece in its own right - as well as providing an excuse for some of those gorgeous industrial locomotives from High Level Models kits.

As is often the case with this type of layout, the trackwork includes a lot of curved or otherwise 'customised' turnouts and would benefit greatly from hand-laying, particularly if the pre-group period was being considered. NER track is very distinctive, using relatively small and unobtrusive chairs and often ballasted right to the sleeper-tops with a fine ash/slag ballast - features that give it a very 'smooth' look. Many turnouts also used interlaced timbering (standard-length sleepers laid separately for each road in a turnout rather than continuous point timbers) - another characteristic feature well

worth reproducing. PCB-based track-building techniques have proved admirably suited to modelling NER track.

Although drawn as a home layout, I think this is one of the designs here which could be adapted to exhibition use as well if required, by modifying the background landscape and scenery (which includes a lot of retaining walls, easy to make removable) to make it more suitable as 'foreground'. The real snag would be that you would then have to model all four sides of the buildings; thank goodness there aren't too many of them!

Summary:

Subject: Newcastle and Carlisle line/early BR.

Scale/gauge: 4mm/00 (EM possible).

Site size: 12 x 8 feet.

Ruling curve radius: (Main line) 33" Mineral railway: 24".

Ruling grade: (mineral railway) 1 in 24.

Longest fiddleyard road: 60".

Further reading:

The Newcastle & Carlisle Railway,
by G Whittle. D & C, 1979.
Lord Carlisle's Railways,
by Brian Webb and David Gordon, RCTS 1978 (Excellent!).
Forgotten Railways of North East England,
by Ken Hoole. D & C, 1973.
North Eastern Album, by Ken Hoole. Ian Allan, 1974.

Bodmin Road

Yes, we're back in Cornwall - but where would you rather be on a glorious July day in 1960? Lazing in the sun three-parts of the way up farmer Prouze's new-shorn hayfield with a grandstand view of the summer Saturday goings-on at Bodmin Road was pretty much Valhalla so far as I was concerned. With a packet of cheese-and-pickle sandwiches and a bottle of Dandelion and Burdock to sustain me and the obligatory ABC and notebook for information and recording purposes, the rest of the family could keep the beach at Harlyn or the visit to Tintagel Castle. I was in my element.

In truth, the scene looked not unlike a model railway in itself, with the main line tracks climbing through the narrow wooded valley on a long, sweeping left-hand bend (looking in the up direction) and the branch down the hill from Bodmin town appearing from amid the trees around a flange-squealing curve. There was a compact goods yard beyond the platform-end on the down side, while across in the 'vee' between the main line and the branch was the fan of sidings for the china-clay wagons worked down from Wenford by way of Boscarne Junction.

There always seemed to be activity of some sort at Bodmin Road, even if it was nothing more than the branch 45XX basking by the water tank - which was in itself unique, with its odd aqueduct across the branch tracks to the up main line platform. At various times in the day, another 45XX or perhaps a 57XX pannier would be busy with the clay workings, squealing down the hill amid a groan of brakes at the head of a rake of loaded wagons, or barking off back up the hill to Bodmin with the empties.

But all this, of course, was just the entre-act; it was the main line that provided the serious entertainment. And on a Saturday in the high season, that was train after packed train of the bucket-and-spade brigade journeying to or from their annual pilgrimage to Coverack, Marazion, Mevagissey or Mullion Cove, up over the Downs to Newquay or on to Chacewater for Perranporth and St. Agnes, further west still for St. Erth for St, Ives, Penzance, Newlyn, Land's End or remote Zennor. And yes, I do like Cornish place-names! In the mornings, the predominant traffic was up towards Plymouth, trains destined to head on over the South Devon banks to Exeter, Bristol, the Midlands and even further north, to such remote near-Arctic spots as Manchester, Leeds or Bradford. The up 'Cornish Riviera' - often double headed - appeared just about sandwich-opening time. The down action really picked up after the last lunchtime apple-core had been buried in the hedge-foot, with the down 'Riviera' as the centrepiece in the late afternoon.

Motive power over the Cornwall main line in summer was ever-varied although almost exclusively Great Western in origin. The only non-Swindon interlopers were the handful of 'Britannias' still allocated to the far west - infrequent performers and soon ousted by the throbbing bull-nosed 'Warship' diesels. 'Castles' and 'Counties' were the star turns on the heaviest trains, with double-heading frequent in the 'up' direction; it's a stiff climb up the Glynn Valley from Bodmin to Doublebois, and a packed 15-coach holiday train would rate a pair of 4-6-0s, or at least a 4-6-0 and a Mogul. Mainstay of the service were the Halls and Granges, aided by Manors and Moguls. Local trains were also usually worked by a 4-6-0 (Imagine! A local train worked by a 'namer!') and freight trains (not that there were any on a summer Saturday, except very early in the morning) also usually rated at least a Mogul.

Weekdays were different and although not as frenetic as the full Summer Saturday procession, offered more variety. Passenger trains (still quite frequent) were interspersed with milk and perishables (vegetables from Helston, and a lot of meat wagons from I know not where), parcels trains and regular freights. The faster freight traffic usually had a 'Grange' or 'Hall', while the important London milk trains (early afternoon and mid-evening) were often a 'Castle' or 'County' turn. Slow traffic could be a 28XX, Mogul or 'Grange', or even a tank locomotive - a small or large Prairie, or maybe a pannier tank on the pick-up goods. China-clay trains from Bodmin Road down to Par would be worked by tank engines, too - sometimes, a handsome 42XX from St Blazey shed, or a couple of smaller types like 45 or 57XX. Plenty of variety...

And the model?

Bodmin Road is a surprisingly compact station, nestled deep in the cleft of the valley. The platforms are not over-long - especially on the 'up' side, and even going 'down' it wasn't uncommon for big holiday trains to draw up twice if some poor soul at the rear needed to alight. All of which makes it, in many ways, pretty much a perfect subject for a model railway in a modest space. I have managed to 'squeeze' it down into a 12 x 8 ft site before now, but this slightly more expansive version is on the 14 x 9 Bedroom/attic site, which allows slightly longer trains.

So far as the actual station layout goes, this almost designs itself. There are no major compromises to make other than a spot of compression and a tweak to the curves here and there. I've omitted two clay sidings and moved the trailing crossover at the 'up' end a bit further towards the station. It was actually on the far side of the bridge over the lane, not on the platform ends as shown here. This prototype track plan is the later one, which pertained from about 1960 or so; previously, there had been two trailing connections from the branch onto the up line - the second one (which was on what became simply a head-shunt) allowed clay trains to get out even when there was a passenger train standing at the branch platform. The platforms were of unequal length as depicted - they had both been extended from their original (very short) length but the 'up' platform had to stop short for the junction.

You'll notice that, once again, all turnouts in the running lines are trailing and that there is no direct 'down' connection to the branch; trains needing to go up the hill to Bodmin from the Plymouth direction set back through the crossover and made a 'wrong line' move controlled by ground discs and under the protection of the home and starting signals. Generally speaking, these were clay trains only - passenger workings terminated at Bodmin Road. However, these weren't all shuttles to Bodmin General - some ran around and dropped down the 1 in 37 to Boscarne and onto Southern metals to run on to Wadebridge and Padstow. The clay trains, too, reversed at Bodmin General for the run down to Boscarne, the interchange point with the Wenford Bridge line.

Once again, I've used the ploy of two separate stub-ended fiddleyards to handle longer trains, one for the Plymouth direction and one for 'Down Cornwall'. The longest road in each yard is some 10ft 6ins long, which will take a ten-coach train and two locomotives. These yards are also separated by elevation, with the rear yard being higher by some + 2.5ins. to ease access without disturbing trains in the lower (front) yard. The continuous run drops down from this elevation to datum at the exit to the 'Down Cornwall' yard on a 1 in 40 grade. Emerging from the mouth of Brownqueen tunnel, main line trains climb at the same grade to the entrance to the station, run through the platforms on the level and re-commence the climb beyond junction - all as per prototype. The track through the platforms is at + 1.5ins over datum.

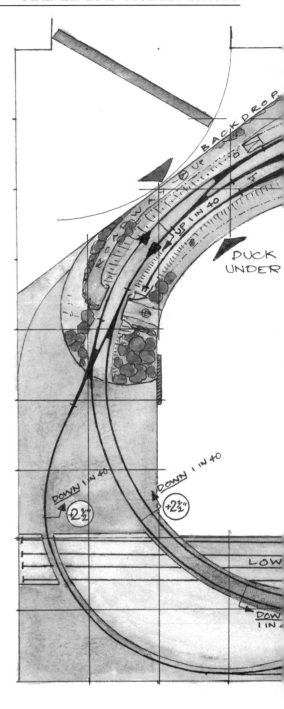

Higher still is the cassette that serves the Bodmin branch, reached by a panting 1 in 30 climb up from the platform end and set some 3.5ins above datum. At around 3 ft. long this will easily handle the 45XX/B Set that was the regular branch passenger train, or about 9 clay wagons, a 45XX and a brake van. The fiddleyards are partly concealed by floor-to-ceiling drapes to match the normal below-baseboard ones; these can be drawn aside for access. Usually, in a second bedroom site, the main window is in a long wall. An attic wouldn't present such a problem, while this layout would go very nicely in a 16 x 9 garage and allow even longer trains - although still not the 'full fifteen' of the prototype

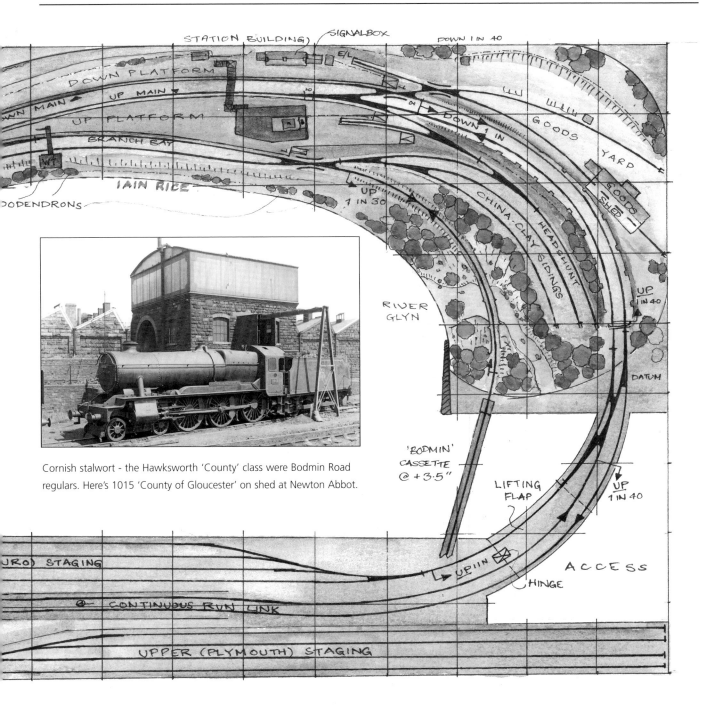

Cornish stalwort - the Hawksworth 'County' class were Bodmin Road
regulars. Here's 1015 'County of Gloucester' on shed at Newton Abbot.

In practical terms, this is really a strict 00 gauge layout and is intended to make good use of current RTR locos - the Castle, County, Hall, Manor, Mogul, large Prairie and pannier tanks are all available, as are excellent Collett 57ft. and BR Mk1 coaches. The notable omissions at present are the Grange and Hawksworth coaching stock on the main line, and the 45XX for the branch. The first is maybe not 'popular' enough, but I would say a decent 'Small Prairie' has got to be in the offing from either Bachmann or Hornby. Bachmann make clay wagons, and the Hornby (née Airfix) 'B' set is quite reasonable.

I had in mind the usual 'mid-range mix' of SMP bullhead flexible track with PCB-based pointwork. As drawn, all the unseen track could be standard Peco except for the entries to the fiddleyards - effectively a turnout and a single slip on a curve, which will probably need making 'in situ'. With a bit of juggling and some adjustment of curve radii, it would be possible to use standard Peco items, but this is the sort of situation where the 'adjustability' of PCB-based pointwork is a boon. I would operate all the Bodmin Road turnouts from a lever frame situated as shown, perhaps using power operation for the five turnouts at the Plymouth end. DCC would suit this layout admirably. Otherwise, it's all pretty straightforward stuff - although I will confess that I haven't yet hit on a good way of modelling Rhododendrons in full flower....

New Hey and Old Hall

BR (M), LMS (L&Y)

The L & Y is one of my favourite pre-group railways - for reasons I can never quite put a finger on - and has many characteristics that make it eminently 'model-logenic', particularly in the context of this book. For a start, none of the L & Y's passenger routes was over-lengthy in terms of distance travelled, and a frequent service of relatively short main line trains pulled by smaller engines was the norm. Only Wakes Week holiday trains to Blackpool or Aintree race specials went to the extremes of loading often seen elsewhere. Even in the LMS period, a 6 - 8 coach main line formation was typical, and a modest 4-6-0 the top end

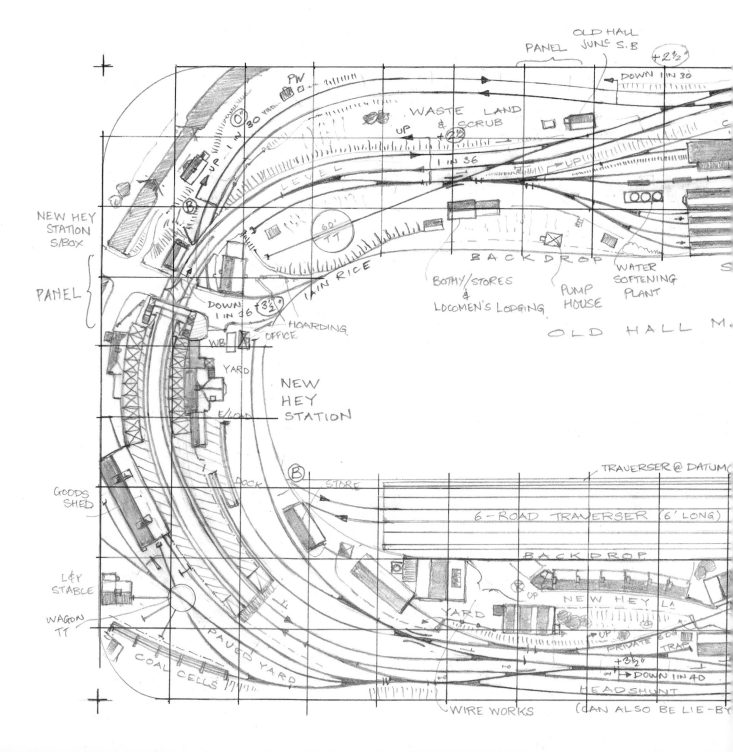

of the passenger power spectrum. Many main-line services in L & Y days were powered by tank engines - the ubiquitous Aspinall 2-4-2T 'Radials' (one of the few tank types fitted with water scoop apparatus) originated as express passenger engines.

Seriously heavy freight was the other trump card in the L & Y hand, and the density of the scheduled freight services is almost unbelievably complex. As well as heavy mineral traffic from the Yorkshire coalfields (hauled by some very handsome 0-8-0 tender engines), there was a major traffic in raw material and finished goods for the cotton,

woollen and general clothing trades, for heavy engineering and chemical industries, paper-making and a whole range of craft trades requiring an intensive parcels service. Plenty of grist, in other works, for the layout-operating mill. And this is above all an operator's layout - designed to be worked, and worked intensively. Well, the old L & Y was; in fact, it was one of the most intensively-worked of pre-group railways, and in the top few in the world both for freight tonnage and passenger train-miles. Remarkable, when you consider what a compact (but complex) system it was. The L & Y also ran a pioneering traffic control scheme from 1915, which for its computerless day was a miracle of line occupancy and intensive rostering.

The layout proposal

Don't bother thumbing your gazeteer for either New Hey 0r Old Hall, Lancashire, because they ain't there. The location for this mid-sized, high-density layout is entirely fictional, although it has some firm prototype roots in New Hall Hey (on the Rawtenstall line, hence the name), Ramsbottom and in the classic small L & Y loco depot at Bacup. New Hey is presumed to be on the Manchester and Leeds section somewhere in the vicinity of Todmorden, and sets out to look as typically L & Y as possible. So there are lots of classic L & Y LDEs included - plenty of over and under bridges, short tunnels, bare rock cuttings, sooty stone embankments and retaining walls. The goods depot at New Hey has coal cells and a 5-way wagon turntable, and there are no less than four typical L & Y signal boxes, as well as a simple through station based on Ramsbottom.

This scheme is primarily designed as a 'high intensity' club or group exhibition/clubroom layout viewable from all four sides. It would need a clear floor area of about 20 x 16 feet (with a reasonable yard of access margin all round) and so could be set up in a domestic double garage. New Hey is intended for full-on prototypical operation using DCC to drive the trains under the control of the four main-line 'signal boxes' which - apart from being modelled - are represented on the layout by four 'on view' control positions incorporating proper lever frames and block instruments. Full and proper

A suitable candidate for Old Hall MPD. The L&Y shed at Ormskirk, Lancs.

working would be both possible and, indeed, necessary if the line potential is to be realised.

There are a lot of grades and levels on this layout, which I've tried to indicate as clearly as possible on the plan. Basically, everything starts from the 0" datum at which the traverser is set - in the context of an exhibition layout, I'd keep this to 42" above floor level or maybe a tad more. A 6-road traverser is shown, but you could go for a bit more capacity as there should be sufficient clearance for the traverser table to slide some way beneath the edge of the upper level at the rear of the New Hey Mills scene.

From the traverser toward New Hey Junction, the line rises at 1 in 36 through the tunnel beneath the large mill, then levels out through the junction itself (which is at an elevation of +1" over datum). The 1 in 36 climb re-commences across the viaduct to reach Old Hall Junction, at a height of +2.5". The main line formation is then level at this height through the loco depot entry before rising once more at 1 in 36 to the summit level of +3.5" over datum, reached at New Hey Station signal box. The route is level through the station and around to a point in front of Crimea Terrace, New Hey, where it drops at about 1 in 40 (all these grades are approximate and can be adjusted a little either way) back down to the +1" elevation at New Hey Junction.

At the opposite end of the traverser, the track runs level at datum below the +3.5" level of New Hey Station, and then climbs at a steep 1 in 30 to reach the 'return junction' at Old Hall. The severity of all these grades could be reduced considerably by using minimal headroom (+2.25") over the trackage below New Hey station; with a thin baseboard surface at this point and framing arranged to maintain full headroom above the low-level track, you could take as much as an inch out of the height differential between datum and New Hey Station, which should put all the grades on the right side of 1 in 40. But at the cost of difficult access to the low-level trackage...

Traffic would include express passenger workings, local stopping passenger, heavy minerals, general freight, pick-up goods trains and parcels workings. The layout could be realised in EM, as the curves are generally 3ft radius or above, and no particularly large or long rigid-wheelbase locos are required. The 4mm (and 3mm if it comes to it) L & Y modeller is actually well-served for kits, particularly the old George Norton range - now available from London Road Models in 4mm and the 3mm Society at the smaller size. The range includes the Aspinall 2-4-2 radial tanks (short and long bunker versions), '23' class 0-6-0ST, the Barton Wright 'Ironclad' 0-6-0 tender engine from which the '23s' were rebuilt, and the 30/31 class small and large-boiler 0-8-0s. Craftsman do the Aspinall 'A' class 0-6-0 goods, while the 'Pug' can be had RTR from Dapol/Hornby. For the more dedicated constructor, Falcon

Brass also list a few L & Y locos including the Aspinall steam railmotor and the 0-6-0 'Rapid Shunting Tank'. There is also a good selection of L & Y coaches in both scales, from Mallard/Blacksmith and D & S Models. D & S will also sell you the characteristic 'Tin Tabernacle' brake van, while David Geen/51L, D & S Models and ABS have a good selection of L & Y goods stock.

L & Y locomotives were long-lived, so all of the above engines would suit the LMS/early BR periods. That would also permit later L & Y-designed but LMS-built types such as the Hughes 'Baltic Tank' and the revised 'Dreadnought' 4-cylinder 4-6-0 (Millholme), and not forgetting - of course - the immortal and hugely successful 'Crab' 2-6-0 (Bachmann RTR, and quite superb!) Foreigners seen after 1923 were usually of LNWR origin or derivation, such as the 'Patriot' 4-6-0s. For the later LMS and BR periods, the Stanier standard 4-6-0s were prevalent, along with the 8F and 'Jinty' designs. LMS 4Fs also appeared on freight workings, where they were suffered by Horwich men used to something a little more manly. But, wisely, the LMS rarely inflicted the feebler Midland types on so stern a route. Goodness knows what the Lanky would have made of a Derby 'sewing machine' job.

Summary:

Subject: L & Y/LMS/BR (M) in East Lancashire.
Scale/gauge: 4mm/00, EM possible.
Site size: 14 x 10 exhibition layout, 20 x 16 room required.
Ruling curve radius: 36".
Ruling grade: 1 in 30.
Longest fiddleyard road: 72" (6-coach express + 4-6-0).

Further Reading:

The Lancashire & Yorkshire in the 20th. Century,
by Eric Mason (one of the truly great railway books).
Ian Allan, 1954/61.
The Lancashire and Yorkshire Railway (FDetailed History), Vols 1 - 3,
by John Marshall. D & C, 1968 - 72.

- or, for an overview:

The Lancashire and Yorkshire Railway - A Concise History,
by O S Nock, Ian Allan, 1969.
Railway History in Pictures - North-West England,
by John Clarke and J Allen Patmore. D & C, 1970
L & Y 150,
by Noel Coates. Hawkshill Publishing/L & Y Society 1997.
LMS Engine Sheds Vol 3 - the Lancashire & Yorkshire Railway,
by Chris Hawkins and George Reeve. Wild Swan, 1982.
Scenes from the past 33 - East Lancashire Lines:
Bury to Heywood and Rawtenstall,
by Jeffrey Wells and Eric Bentley. Foxline, 1999.
(Good plans and excellent photos)

Witham Junction in N Scale

Witham Junction and the West Yard in N

There are plenty of main-line prototypes where the freight workings are as important - in traffic terms - as the passenger trains, but precious few where they're as glamorous. The notable exception in modern times has been provided by the unit mineral trains worked - with their own, trend-setting, state-of-the-art power - by Foster Yeoman quarries and, subsequently, by Mendip Rail, a pragmatic pooling of rail transport arrangements between Foster Yeoman and Ameys, the other big player in the aggregate/roadstone business. In the last fifteen or so years, these big stone trains have become an established aspect of our railways, and are among the most impressive spectacles to be seen anywhere on what we must now call Network Rail.

It was Foster Yeoman who effectively first blazed the trail with what is now the norm on our railways (and subsequently many elsewhere in Europe) - privately-owned trains using a publicly-owned network. Foster Yeoman had railways in their bloodline, the original working opened by Foster Yeoman, Esq in 1923 at Dulcoate near Wells being adjacent to the GWR branchline and ballast quarries and hence allied to the use of rail transport from the outset. When the huge new quarries at Merehead were being developed in the early 1970s rail also figured in the initial transport arrangements, with a new link being built from the stone loading terminal to a trailing junction at Cranmore, on that same ex-GWR branch - which once ran on through Cheddar and up the Axe Valley to Yatton Junction on the Bristol & Exeter main line.

The heavy Merehead stone traffic was worked out to the junction at Cranmore, where the trains reversed to run over the eastern stump of the old branch to Witham, junction with the GWR West of England main line. Thence, the stone went forward over BR to distribution depots in the London area and, subsequently, throughout much of southern Britain. The trains were pushed out to the BR trackage by FY's own power (originally ex-BR 08

shunters running in multiple, later aided by a hulking great American EMD SW1001 switcher) then worked onward by contemporary BR power - mostly Warship, Western and Hymek class diesel hydraulics. In more recent years, a sharply curved connection facing Witham has been put in at Merehead so that empty trains can run direct to the loading point, while the loaded trains are pushed out to Cranmore by main-line power.

As the operation built up, the various BR locomotives became less and less able to cope with the weight and volume of traffic. Availability suffered as the strain proved too much for what were, at best 'mixed traffic' engines, not really designed for the sort of heavy 'drag freight' that the stone traffic represented. The arrival of the similarly mixed-traffic class 47 didn't help much, and it was only when the 3,250hp type 56 freight diesels became available in the early 1980s that FY could start to run the sort of 'super train' they were after - 30 or more 102-ton bogie hoppers grossing 3,000+ tons. These were train weights then completely unprecedented in Britain, and they placed a new set of demands on the operating department.

The 56s and later 58s could do the job - working in pairs - but not with notable reliability or adequate availability. Lack of locomotive power and train paths for the greater number of smaller trains being run soon began to impede Foster Yeoman's business development. So, after long discussions with BR, FY took the bold step of doing their own thing and commissioning a completely new locomotive design from EMD (Electro-Motive Division of General Motors) specifically for their traffic, based on the outstandingly successful six-axle SD40 - 2 design developed for heavy long-distance freight trains in the USA. This commission was actually quite a tall order - or rather, quite a short one; the British loading gauge is far, far smaller than that in the US and the maximum axle loading much lower, so it was very far from a case of simply sticking a set of buffers on an SD40 and shipping it off to Somerset.

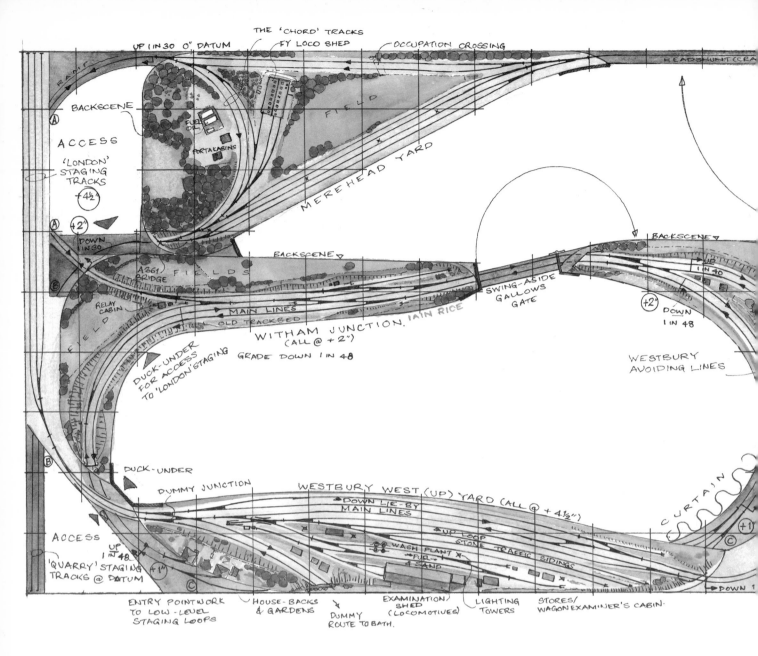

The result was a completely new design based around the 3,300hp turbocharged V-16 power unit of the SD40, incorporating all the sophisticated computer-controlled traction and anti-wheelslip technology of the -2 version and riding on the same articulated self-steering bogies - but in a locomotive that was smaller, lighter and faster than the US version. The class 59, as BR classified the interloper, was an outstanding success, and in the developed version (Class 66) seems set fair to become not only the premier British freight diesel but also the pan-European standard. They are also, in my opinion, just about the most charismatic new piece of power to appear in Britain since the original HST of 1972.

The best of modern British in N

I suppose I have to own up to not being much of a fan of many aspects of contemporary British railways. The machinations of the politicians and the accountants have, it seems

to me, brought what was once the world's finest rail network more-or-less to its knees, and most of my recent experiences of travelling by train have been - well, shall we just say 'disappointing'? It was on one such trip, a few years ago, that I found myself disgorged from a stuffy, overcrowded and late-running 'First Great Western' HST (Is Sir James Milne spinning in his grave at the debasing of that great title, I wonder?) at Reading. I had some time to wait for my onward connection so, with an hour to kill, I wandered up to the 'country' end of the station, where the Berks and Hants line rejoins the original Brunel main line to Bristol, to see if there was anything interesting to look at. And here, held by signals on the former, I lit upon a Mendip Rail '59' at the head of an Acton-bound stone train.

It was the first opportunity I'd had to really study one of these engines at relatively close quarters. I'd read about them of course, seen plenty of pictures of them, passed them on the line or glimpsed them - fleetingly - idling at Westbury or

Theale. But this was the first time I had met one 'in the flesh' with time to take it in, to just stand and stare at it. They're oddly proportioned locomotives, in a way that makes them appear long and sleek and somehow quite petite - although in point of fact they are among the largest diesels to operate in Britain. They are also - amid a mass of essentially derivative designs - quite unique. There's nothing else remotely like them either here or, as far as I'm aware, in the USA - except perhaps some of the machinery dreamed up for 'Star Wars'. I found the sight reminiscent of the 'culture shock' occasioned by the Bullied Q1 and Pacific, while the resmblance to the same designer's 'Leader' class is almost uncanny. But, over-all, I found much to appreciate in what I saw.

In the fullness of time, a path opened up for the stone train and the signals cleared. In spite of being held on a sharp curve and on an adverse grade, the way that the '59' took hold of its load and pulled cleanly away, with a 'thoroughbred throb' from those 16 cylinders but otherwise with no excess of noise, smoke or fuss was impressive. Awesome, even, as the laden bogie stone wagons clattered ever-faster over the junction in an accelerating crescendo. It may lack the drama of steam - or even older diesels - but these GM locomotives exude that sense of power and presence that is notably lacking from so much modern machinery, no matter how potent it might be. They get my vote.

The stone trains are the only services running in Britain that come anywhere near the size and scope of the sort of thing one sees in the USA - although the experimental 12,000-ton 'mega-train' was let down by the design and strength of traditional British link couplers. But loads of 4,500 tons are now commonplace with '59' power - big trains in anybody's book, and hence most readily replicated in N scale. Various versions of the '59' have been available in resin or etched-brass kit form in N to fit the Farish class 56 drivetrain, and Bachmann/Farish have now announced an RTR EW & S Class 66 that will presumably appear decorated in FY or Amey/Mendip Rail colours and backdated as a 59 in due course. So a key factor in modelling the stone trains is to hand.

What is not quite so readily come by is the accompanying rolling stock, especially the big Orenstein & Koppel 102-ton PHA hoppers (79 tonnes of payload) for the bulk traffic to terminals like Acton or Theale. Taylor Plastic models do offer a kit for the later O & K PTA 'Tub' wagons designed for tippler or scoop unloading, while Farish make the older 51-ton 4-wheeled PGA hopper in Yeoman, Amey and Caib (the rolling stock lessor for much of the stone fleet) colours. These are useful wagons, although they are are being phased out now or cascaded to lesser workings like those to Meldon Quarry, Okehampton. The German-built vehicles are very similar to those bogie hoppers running on the DB, and many British modellers simply repaint

Minitrix German 1:160 vehicles to a fair likeness of the smaller British variant in 1:148.

Stone is a very heavy commodity for its bulk, so these are not particularly long vehicles; even so, the 45 of them making up a 4600-ton unit train is quite a lengthy affair; from the lineside, it can take a good couple of minutes to trundle past . Fortunately, not all stone from the Mendips moves in these super-trains, and much more modest formations of 10 - 15 vehicles are not uncommon. 15 N scale PHA hoppers, according to my calculator, scales at at around the 60-inch mark in N; say five-and-a-half feet with the loco - not too impossible, and easily compatible with the 7-car West of England HST sets that provide most of the passenger service over these metals. However, I wanted to be able to impress with at leat a 'low-end supertrain', so the longest 'London' fiddleyard siding is designed to take a 20-wagon formation, which at least looks impressive!

Otherwise, this is a conventional enough layout in the 'stationless genre' - Frome off on its loop is completely ignored - as is the running line from Witham to Westbury, telescoped into the eighteen inches of the swing-aside gallows entry gate - while Westbury is represented by the western approaches only in this scheme. (The plan shown here is extracted from a far more ambitious scheme, an American-style basement-busting affair covering the whole route from Merehead to Theale and entitled - in best US parlance - the 'Westbury Sub'; but this does not occupy - by any definition of the term - a 'modest space'!) As well as the stone line from Witham to Cranmore and into the quarry at Merehead, the present layout serves up a slice of the main line, the traction depot at Westbury and some of the marshalling facilities, plus one end of the Westbury Avoiding Line. Ok, this is by no stretch of the imagination an accurate rendition of the real Westbury, but I think it has the right 'feel' even if some of the elements are out of place. With HST sets still running on the main line, and classes 56, 59, 60 and 66 on the stone trains, it presents a contemporary railway scene with more presence than most - but still in that modest space.

Summary:

Subject: BR West of England main line/late 1990s.
Scale/gauge: N.
Site size: 14 x 9 feet.
Ruling curve radius: 15" (on stone branch) 24" on main line.
Ruling grade: 1 in 30 (hidden, on branch).
Longest fiddleyard road: Main line - 8 feet; 'London' 6ft 6ins.

Further reading:

Foster Yeoman - the Rail Album 1923 -1998,
by Hugh Searle & Robin Jacob.
Pub by Foster Yeoman. (Available through Challis Models & Hobbies, 50B High St, Shepton Mallet, Somerset, BA4 5AS.)

Binegar, S & D
Over the Mendips in 4mm

The S & D has long been a subject popular with modellers, and with good reason. It was a very individual railway with an unusual mix of traffic types and a demanding route, partly single-track. It ran through spectacular and beautiful countryside over some stonking grades, had attractive buildings, imposing viaducts and bridges, and a couple of thoroughly unhealthy tunnels. It was a line which, like the M & GN to which it was in many ways closely related, maintained a great degree of independence - in spite of technically being 'Joint' (the partners in this case being the Midland and the LSWR). It carried a heavy mineral traffic in lime and coal originating in the Mendip area, and was an important route for through traffic from the midlands and north to the south coast resorts, most notably Bournemouth.

And, of course, the S & D had that vital asset of any railway aspiring to main line status - long-distance, named express trains. In this case, none other than the immortal 'Pines Express' (Manchester to Bournemouth) and the less-well-known 'North Express' (from Bradford/Leeds). Working such heavy trains over a route containing tortuous curves and many a mile graded well on the steeper side of 1 in 100 - quite a bit of it at 1 in 50 - was no sinecure. Even though the line's motive power affairs were essentially dictated by the Midland's small-engine policy, the S & D was an early user of 8-coupled power, in the form of the distinctive 2-8-0s built specially for the line from 1914. These engines later carried on the S & D tradition of working heavy passenger trains with freight locos - culminating in the success of the BR 9F 2-10-0 in the last few years of the 'Pines'.

The S & D was another line I was lucky enough to know well in the swansong years of the later 1950s. (Sorry about all these nostalgic ramblings and reminiscences - but there have to be a few compensations for reaching that age at which one starts sliding downhill into one's dotage...). Ours was a family much given to farmhouse holidays, and Thrupe Farm at Masbury was the favoured destination from about 1955 - 58. High (over 800' above sea level) on the open, airy spaces of the Mendips, just below the long ramparts of iron-age Maesbury Castle (or

'Ring'), Thrupe was a lovely spot - the more so because the S & D main line bisected the farm only about a hundred yards from the end of the farmhouse we occupied. The actual summit of the whole S & D climb over the Mendips was right by the occupation bridge that linked the 'Home Fields' with the rest of the farm - a perfect spot for train-watching, where the banking engines dropped off (of which more in a moment).

It was on the S & D that I first met the Bullied light pacifics - just one class amid the wide variety of engines that could be seen on the workings over the Mendips at that time. As well as the air-smoothed pacifics (quite a few of which came to the S & D brand-new) there were a goodly number of S & D survivors including 'Bulldogs' (the S & D version of the MR Deeley class 3F), 'Armstrongs' (similar to the later MR 4Fs but built by Armstrong-Whitworth, hence the name), 'Superheaters' (basically the MR Deeley class 2 4-4-0 design) and, of course, the splendid 'eight-coupled goods'. There were also 'Jinties' - a mix of ex-S & D Bagnall-built engines and standard LMS examples - plus LMS stalwarts such as the 4F 0-6-0, Stanier Class 5 4-6-0, Ivatt's type 4 2-6-0 and the same designer's 2-6-2T. BR standards were also in evidence - the class 4 and 5 4-6-0s, the occasional class 4 Mogul or type 3 2-6-2T. The 9Fs and Standard class 4 2-6-4T didn't appear until after my time, in the early 1960s. The GWR got into the act with several Collet 2251 0-6-0s, while various Southern classes could appear - T9s and Moguls particularly. Quel embarras de richesse!

The trains were equally variegated. As well as BR Mk 1 stock in just about any livery - green, maroon, chocolate-and-cream or classic blood-and-custard - there was a goodly mix

A typical Somerset and Dorset summer working on the climb up to Masbury summit, headed by a classic S & D locomotive combination - a Bulleid pacific piloted by a 2P.
Author's Collection.

of pre-nationalisation types, especially from the Southern and Midland regions. SR Bullied and Maunsell stock ran with the earler panelled or later flush-sided LMS stock, various Gresley designs from the Eastern Region, and the odd GW Collett or Hawksworth coach. About the only thing you didn't usually see were Pullmans! The through trains varied in length from around 6 to 11 coaches (double-headed); locals were 2 - 4 coach affairs, ex-GW 'B Sets' or BR standard steel-sided suburbans, even some pre-group panelled compartment stock - Midland, I suppose. Freight was also pretty variegated and rarely over-long. Even the 2-8-0s were limited to a couple of dozen loads, with a Radstock or Templecombe 'Jinty' giving vigorous assistance over the steep bit.

Mendip in Miniature

This layout design, intended for a single-garage or attic site, is based on the last section of the southbound climb, from Binegar Station to Masbury Summit (811 feet). This is not only the bit of the line I knew best, but it was also the subject of an interesting and uncommon working practice, the use of a 'banking key'. While the normal practice was to pilot passenger trains between Bath and Evercreech, goods trains were always banked 'over the hill'. Going south, the banking engine came on at Radstock and in the other direction at Evercreech. Although this was a double-track section of line, the actual summit at Masbury lay in the middle of a block (Binegar - Masbury). In earlier times, Masbury Station signal box was normally manned - so southbound banking engines could drop off there and set back through the station crossover to return to Radstock on the 'up' line. In later years, however, Masbury was usually 'switched out'. This didn't affect northbound trains, as the banker simply ran through to Binegar, where the box was continuously manned, and used the crossover there to return to Evercreech 'right line'. But going south the next available crossing point was at Shepton Mallet, half-way back down the 'wrong side' of the hill.

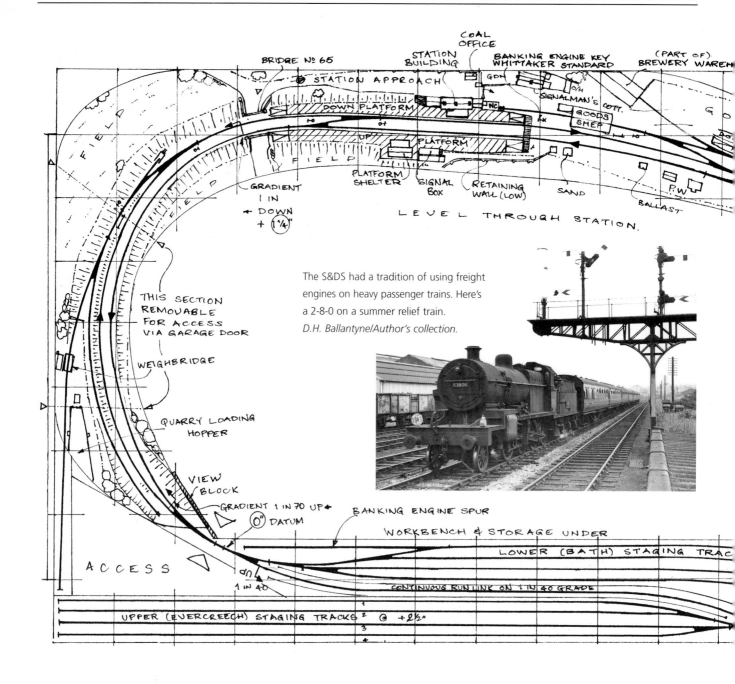

The S&DS had a tradition of using freight engines on heavy passenger trains. Here's a 2-8-0 on a summer relief train.
D.H. Ballantyne/Author's collection.

So, to avoid excessive line occupancy and engine mileage, a slightly unusual working practice was adopted for southbound trains. The banker pushed up to the summit but dropped off once the train was safely 'over the hill' - a hundred yards or so beyond the Thrupe Farm occupation bridge - and returned to northwards to Binegar, still on the down line. At Binegar was that trailing crossover, which enabled the banking engine to cross to the 'up' line and hence regain normal running. This operation was under the protection of the banking key - a form of token authorising total line occupation of one road of a double-track route. The home signal in the rear of the occupied section could only be cleared when the 'key' was in the signalbox as it was necessary to 'unlock' the signal lever - although the cleared signal could always be returned to

'danger'. So if the key was carried on the banker like a train staff or token on a single line, the move was protected from following traffic; this could not be admitted to the section until the banking key was back in the signalbox.

Although the climb eased a little through Binegar - sited on a grade of 1 in 178 - it steepened to 1 in 63 once the station was passed. Obviously, it was undesirable to stop or slow trains for manual banking key exchange in such circumstances, so this was accomplished by a modified form of the Whittaker Automatic Tablet Exchange Apparatus, as used to work the single-track parts of the line. A 'catcher' on the loco collected the key from a lineside standard without any need to slow down (not that the speeds involved were ever much more than about 20 mph anyway!). When the banker returned to

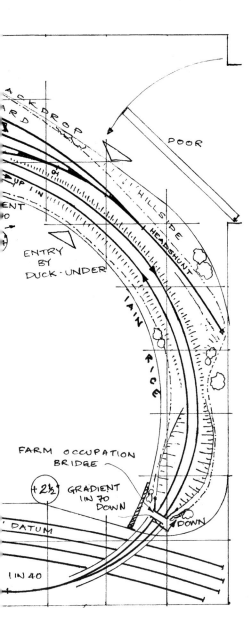

To fit Binegar into the garage, I've used the usual tricks of compression and curve tightening, but once again the fundamental track layout remains true to the original even if it is not quite all there (a couple of sidings and some sheds beyond the cattle dock are missing). The station - like the prototype, on a grade - occupies one side of the garage and the tracks continue up the grade to Masbury Summit and to the upper 'southbound' staging yard on the opposite garage wall. North of Binegar, the tracks continue to drop downgrade past the quarry sidings (where in reality there was a brief stretch of level track) to enter the low-level staging. This is arranged so that only the longest roads lie beneath the approach to upper level yard. There's a linking track that drops from the upper to the lower yards to provide a continous run; as there is no need for 'access clearance' to the lower staging, the difference in levels is held to the minimum required for one track to cross another - 2.5 inches. The longest road in each staging yard is designed to handle a 10-coach train with two engines, while the ruling curve of 3ft radius should allow EM standards to be used if required.

This is a layout which really would benefit from DCC, not only facilitating the banking operations, but also simplifying the 'parking arrangements' in the staging yard. Operation is not dissimilar to Rowtor, except that it's bankers and not pilots that are being handled (although if Evercreech was short of engines pilots could also be detached at Binegar and sent back for further duties, the line to Bath being all 'downhill' apart from the short stretch of 1 in 100 from Midford up to Coombe Down Tunnel). Roll on the advent of onboard sound and other such digital sophistications (automatic Bullied wheel-slip, perhaps?); this is the sort of layout which would take on an extra dimension if one could hear as well as see the trains toiling up-grade.

Summary:

Subject: S & DJR/BR Period c1960.
Scale/gauge: 4mm, 00 or EM.
Site size: 16 x 9 feet.
Ruling curve radius: 36".
Ruling grade: 1 in 60.
Longest fiddleyard road: 10ft 3ins.

Further reading:

The Somerset and Dorset Railway,
by Robin Atthill/O S Nock. D & C, 1967.
Somerset and Dorset Locomotive History,
by Bradley & Milton. D & C, 1973.
A Picture History of the Somerset and Dorset Railway,
by Robin Atthill. D & C, 1970.
Mendips Engineman,
by P W Smith and Ivo Peters. OPC, 1972.

Binegar, the key was given up to the signalman once the banker was safely on the 'up' line and the crossover restored. All very modellable!

Binegar was otherwise a typical S & D wayside station, with the added bonus of the Mendips Stone Works sidings at the 'up' end. There was also a sizeable goods yard which, among other commodities, handled the output of the Oakhill Brewery. This once had its own steam-worked narrow-gauge (3ft) rail link to the brewery itself, some two miles distant. This explains the presence of two goods sheds at Binegar - the normal modest railway-company edifice, and a very large stone building that was effectively the brewery's warehouse. As usual, the running lines are devoid of facing points, although there is a trailing single slip to liven things up.

Yeoford Junction
Made for modelling...

When casting about for inspiration for layout design proposals, one is apt - I fear - to overlook that which is on the proverbial doorstep. Well, if not actually on the doorstep, then still the right side of the garden gate - such as this version of Yeoford Junction, on the Exeter - Barnstaple line, little more than a brisk twenty-minute drive from the fairey battlements of El Casa Rice. I remarked on the SR Exeter-Barnstaple route as being definitely 'main line' in ambience back in my pre-ramble, and to me it always has been. It's those Bullied pacifics, you see, which seem to have figured greatly in my youth and adolescence. To me - ignorant of their true status as powerful, lightweigh mixed-traffic engines - they were the very epitome of modern main line power. So any route that boasted Bullieds became, Ipso Facto, an Important Railway in Rice's book. But then, a route which was once home to the magnificence of the Devon Belle - all Pullman with observation car - must surely have some claim to premium status?

The Exeter-Barnstaple line was another of those puzzling railways - like the Somerset and Dorset aforementioned - which mixed an intensely rural setting and considerable single-track mileage with named main-line trains and a surprisingly heavy traffic. To stand on the platform at Yeoford today (thankfully you still can, although all you can hope for by way of a train is a rattly old Regional Railways type 155 on the 'Tarka Line' service - yeuch!), one is hard put to it to see this as anything but a remote railway backwater, hanging on to its 'still open' status by the veriest thread. The tranquilty and rusticity of today hold little hint of the bustle that characterised the place on summer weekends gone by, when the 'Withered Arm' Plymouth and North Cornwall lines diverged at Coleford, a mile or so further west. They still do - although the arm doesn't even get to the elbow (Halwill?) these days, being cut short at the eastern end of Meldon's spindly viaduct, a couple of miles beyond Okehampton. However, the stretch of this line from Sampford Courtenay to Meldon does now carry Dartmoor Railway tourist trains for much of the

year, and Okehampton Station has been beautifully restored - among other things, it houses my local model shop. Very handy.

In its pre-1960 heyday, Yeoford was a busy place indeed. When one realises that the "Atlantic Coast Express" and its various relief sections could amount to as much as three or four separate trains in each direction - sometimes heavy enough to be double-headed - one begins to get a flavour of the 'main line' ambience of the place, even if the Devon Belle had by then bowed out. As well as various sections of the 'up' ACE, regular holiday trains were scheduled for through running from Padstow, Bude, Ilfracombe, Barnstaple to Waterloo, with half a dozen such workings in the span of little more than an hour in the afternoon. These express and holiday workings were in addition to the regular local services to Barnstaple, Ilfracombe, Plymouth and North Cornwall.

There were also important non-passenger perishables traffics - the long-distance milk trains from Torrington were often a 'Pacific' turn, and there was meat from Eggesford and Halwill, fish from Padstow, rabbits from Bridestowe and market-garden produce (especially strawberries in season) from the upper Tamar Valley. The line carried a heavy local milk traffic, with creameries at Torrington and Lapford receiving supplies from all over the North Devon area. Meldon Quarry generated a heavy stone traffic, while timber and timber products came from Chappelton and a considerable volume of general

How could one doubt the main-line status of a line that carried a train like this? The all-Pullman 'Devon Belle', with observation car, ran out the full length of the North Devon line to Ilfracombe. The usual post-war formation was 7-8 cars behind a light Pacific - an eminently modellable train.
Author's Collection.

freight from Barnstaple, which is still an important industrial centre today. China clay and the distinctive cream Marland bricks came up from the North Devon clayfields around Meeth and Peter's Marland, south of Torringtom on the North Devon and Cornwall Junction line. Outward agricultural produce and livestock traffics also featured heavily across the area. Going the other way was coal for the power station at Fremington (on the Torrington line), feed, fertiliser and other agricultual supplies, general merchandise and manufactured goods.

A model Yeoford

Yeoford Junction is, on the whole, a very manageable proposition in model form, meeting a goodly number of the desiderata set out in my opening chapters. It's on a curve, has platforms of modest length (including a bay to serve local train workings), is pleasantly situated amid hilly country, and by way of a bonus possesses a small marshalling yard where traffic for the two main routes was split or consolidated. Indeed,

Yeoford was an important interchange point for traffic being worked from North to South Devon via the Southern; this was the only north-south rail artery between Plymouth and North Devon if you disregard the North Devon and Cornwall Junction, little more than a tortuously-twisty light railway at the best of times.

The snag with Yeoford is that it's a bit on the long-and-thin side, but a combination of the usual truncation plus a bit of tinkering with the curves gets around that in the context of this garage or attic-sized design. It's drawn for the older 16 x 9ft single garage, but if the site were is a tad larger then that would be a huge bonus. There are symetrical separate stub-ended cassette fiddleyards - fifty inches long - for each direction, fed via a turnout and single slip arrangement to serve both the 'up' and 'down' roads of the continuous run. These cassette yards handle the local passenger traffic (up to four coaches and a pacific) and freight workings (up to loco + 12 wagons + brake van). Extra cassettes are racked below the baseboard.

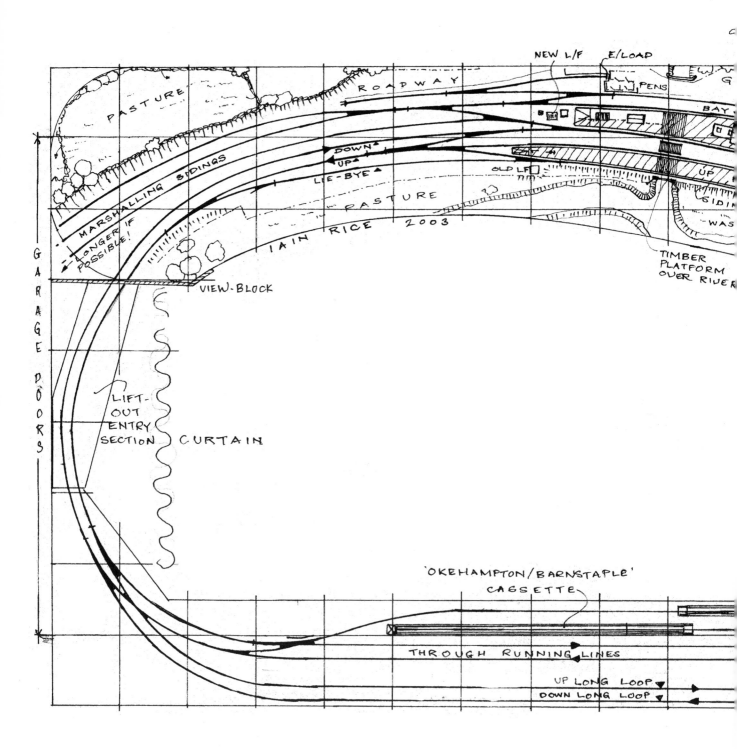

The 50-inch cassettes can be made up of a number of shorter units, dependent on train configuration. On the outside of the continuous run are two long loops - again, one for each direction - which will take a full-length passenger formation - 2 locos and 10 coaches.

This version of Yeoford is quite a faithful copy of the real thing, with a bit of added curvature at no extra charge. The curves all go the right way - they're just a heck of a lot tighter than they should be. Everything is too short, of course, although not as dramatically as is often the case. Yeoford has some peculiarities, all reproduced here - most notably, the wider-than-usual spacing of the tracks through the platforms. This was a legacy of broad gauge days on the North Devon Railway (which started life as the 7ft gauge Exeter and

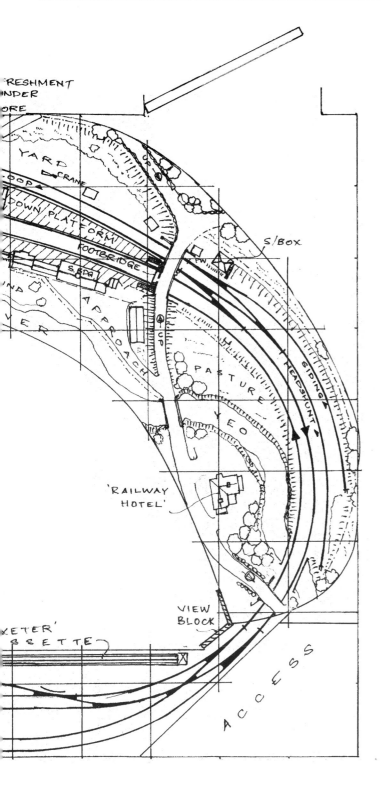

on the Barnstaple side of the road bridge, and the series of bridges over the side-stream of the River Yeo that fall right in the middle of the platforms.

This is one layout I feel would benefit enormously from handlaid trackwork - not because of any special formations or other technical jiggery-pokery, but simply because the real thing is full of subtle curves - very gently curved turnouts, narrow-angle wyes and so on. Looking at photos of Yeoford, there's hardly a 'normal' straight turnout to be seen. I feel that this continuous subtle curvature in P & C work is one of the true 'signature' features of much British PW, and getting that 'flowing look' to the track not only delights the eye, but makes things run much more smoothly to boot. I find there's no substitute for the eye and trackwork built 'in situ' to capture this quality, something I've found all-but impossible using 'standard' point templates or ready-made turnouts. In this case, PCB sleepering with SMP plain track would probably be the way to go for either 00 or EM; the great advantage of PCB-based pointwork is that it's pretty well infinitely adjustable - just the job for a bit of subtle tweaking to get that alignment 'just so'. The two double junctions and the point+slip cassette entries in the fiddleyard would also benefit from custom-building, to maximise fiddleyard occupancy.

So far as the trains go, the 1955 - 1960 timeframe I have in mind can accommodate all the old favourites: Bullied light pacifics, SR 'N' moguls, T9s, Ivatt type 2 2-6-2Ts, BR standard class 4 2-6-4Ts, M7s, even - up to mid 1958 - the last of the Adams '0395' class goods engines. Diesels seen after the demise of steam included TOPS classes 31, 33, 47 and even 50 as well as the inevitable DMUs. The RTR makers serve the builder of this line well - so a T9 or two is probably and maybe the odd M7 are the only kits you'll need to build. Wait long enough and Bachmann will probably oblige anyway! As for the 'Devon Belle' - well, those new Hornby Pullmans are certainly mighty tempting. Wonder if the observation car figures in their plans?

Summary:

Subject: BR (SR) 1955 - 60.

Scale/gauge: 4mm, 00 or EM.

Site size: 16 x 9ft single garage.

Ruling curve radius: 36".

Ruling grade: flat.

Longest fiddleyard road: 11 feet.

Further reading:

Southern Main Lines - Exeter to Barnstaple.
Mitchell & Smith, Middleton Press 1993.
More Southern Steam in the West Country,
by Fairclough & Wills. Bradford Barton, 1975.
The Withered Arm - see notes for Port Isaac Road.

Crediton Railway, a line leased originally by the Bristol and Exeter. The LSWR got in on the act by some rather dubious dealing in Exeter & Crediton shares and eventually succeeding in booting the B & E out - but not before Parliament had insisted that the line onwards to Barnstaple and Bideford was built to accommodate broad gauge trains.) Other Yeoford quirks include a signal box perched high on the cutting-side

Rutford Market
Sherwood Section

It's nice, every now and then, to let down what little hair one still has left and design something just for the hell of it, with no serious finescale or scholarly intent. A pure 'model railway', simply intended to be fun to build, fun to look at, and fun to operate. Over the years, I've amused myself in this way by coming up with my own 'take' on some of the classic model railways of the past - most notably, Norman Eagles' coarse-scale 0 gauge, clockwork-driven 'Sherwood Section'. My approach to creating a 'New Sherwood' is based on the use of the current RTR 00 standards for track and trains with traditional full signalling, bell codes and lever frames, but using state-of-the-art DCC to 'drive' with. This is a mix of control that in some ways has much in common with clockwork operation. That all would be conducted in accord with the dictates of a the LMS Rule Book and a proper working timetable goes without saying.

The first of these Sherwood fantasies, an alternative 'Nottingham Castle' terminal station, appeared in my last layout design book (Urban Layouts). This time out, I've turned my attention to Rutford (later Rufford - a change possibly wrought by a delicate sensitivity over the 'Rut'?) Market, the principal intermediate town on the Sherwood main line and junction for the lines to Bradcaster and Lincoln. And once again I've gone to town in the old tradition, setting out with a wish-list that included most of the classic 'main line station' ingredients: separate through and platform roads, a wide island platform with the main range of buildings, an over-track booking hall, a separate bay for the North Lincolnshire Light Railway, several signal boxes, an M.P.D. (not too grand...) and a fairly spacious goods depot.

The first thing to say about this good old-fashioned garage stuffed full of model railway is that it makes no pretence to be over-close to reality. While I've nicked prototype features from here and there and stuck - more or less - to the rules of full-size PW design (I think I could justify all my facing points...), the primary purpose of this essay was to exercise the imagination and hopefully to create something with plenty of railway atmosphere and lots of operational possibilities for

several people. As with the clockwork original, Rutford is all about a 'Royal Scot' or 'Jubilee' with eight on blasting through on one of those centre roads, while a stopping train cowers at the platform and a goods rattles by on the other 'slow'.

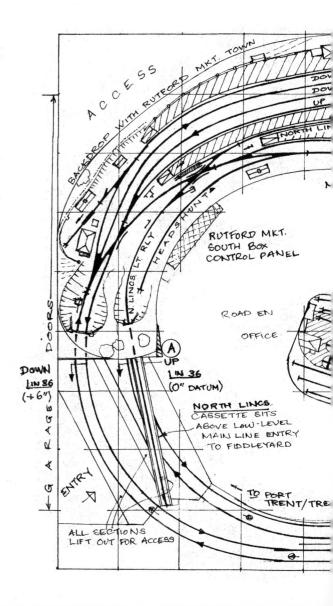

Sherwood solutions

This is one of the larger and more complex layouts that I've designed in a British context (though it would qualify as merely 'mid-sized' in the USA), and is very much intended to make use of all that the trade now offers. Which, for this particular combination of scale, gauge and subject, is plenty. For a start, the trackwork is basically Peco Streamline code 75, with maybe one or two Shinohara curved turnouts (they do a wider range of radii than Peco). In this instance, I think I'd even use Peco's foam ballast inlay, relying on skilful use of the airbrush to make the result look OK; it certainly gives nice, quiet running. As this is very much a DCC-oriented layout, I would bond each length of track back to hefty below-baseboard power busbars to ensure low feed resistance - poor contact (as often occurs when feeding power via rail-joiners) upsets DCC. The layout would also need to be divided into reasonable-sized switched 'blocks' ('Power Districts in DCC-speak) to aid fault-finding.

As an old-fashioned sort of a layout, this exercise uses an old-fashioned format, the 'folded eight', to give a low-level staging yard beneath the main station, connected by long (but relatively steep - to obtain reasonable clearance) offstage grades at each end of the actual station. These grades cross at the 'down' end of Rutford, behind the loco depot, and permit a substantial double-ended ladder staging yard with good train-holding capacity to occupy the same site area as the modelled station. This is an arrangement often used in the USA, and, indeed, was also employed - to good effect - by the late Ken Northwood on the later iterations of the North Devonshire Railway. The only snag on the NDR - located in an outbuilding behind a garage - was that the staging yard was a favoured haunt of spiders, and it was by no means unknown for the 'Torreyman' to burst out of the tunnel leading from the hidden loops with a worried-looking arachnid hanging on to the smokebox!

As these are simply 'staging' - offstage storage loops to hold complete trains - rather than 'fiddle' yards - where trains

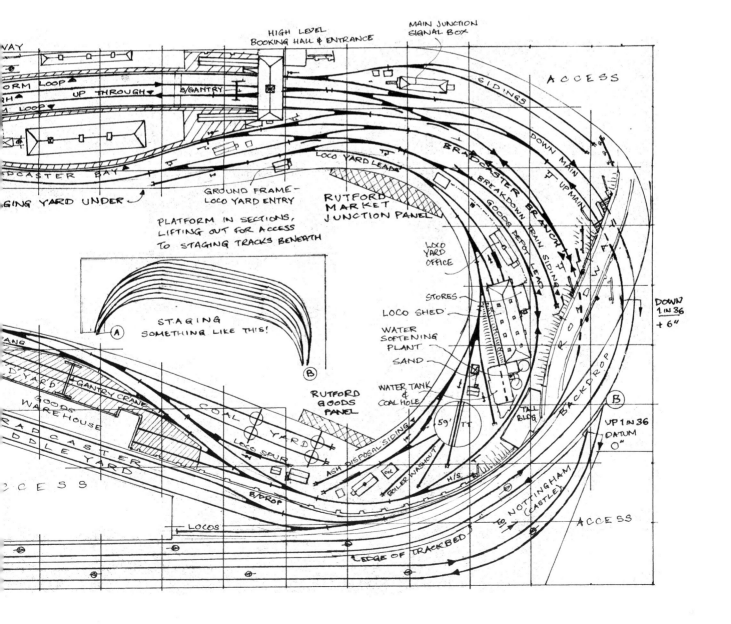

A classic 'Sherwood' loco - an
LMS Jubilee brand new in 1934.
F. Moore/Author's Collection.

A 'Patriot' - LMS power for secondary
main lines. Ideal for Sherwood.
Author's Collection.

are re-marshalled - the comparatively poor access is of lesser importance. I would make the station platforms as a series of lift-out sections fitting between fixed trackbeds, allowing them to be removed for access to the tracks beneath. With reliable locomotives, a well-thought-out route-setting control system for the hidden pointwork and a simple train detection system (IRDOT?), such a system of hidden loops can otherwise be more or less left to their own devices. The North Devonshire staging had a dedicated loop for each train, to give an accurate and consistent match of train to staging road. The hidden system used electric pencil point control on a separate panel, with reed switches operated by magnets on locos and beneath brake vans to give train locations. Simple dead sections with an over-ride push button made sure that engines always stopped in the right place - the only critical factor. This is a 'fail safe' system that works just as well in a DCC context as with conventional control.

Being an old-fashioned operator's model railway, Rutford doesn't waste any precious space on lavish scenic effects - the modelling more-or-less stops at the lineside fence. Which is just as well, as there would be enough to do on the constructional front without having to worry about lots of extraneous structures or landscaping. The signalling, for a start, is going to be no mean feat in its own right, while the point control system would also be a tall order. Although I very much like mechanical point and signal operating systems, I think that in this case the complexity would defeat me; with Peco points, I'd go for their point motors clipped on beneath, with simple solenoid (adapted relay) operation for signals. The 'lever frames' would thus be banks of switches - correctly arranged and colour-coded to accord with a mechanical frame, of course. The wiring would be fearsome, but nowhere near as formidable as the equivalent mechanical linkages.

Otherwise, this layout is simply a setting for the best of modern British RTR. With a mid/late-1930s setting (as on the original Sherwood) the shopping list would be easy (if long!), with Bachmann's exquisite new 'Crab' and Hornby's Class 5 at the top of the page. Just about everything you would need to equip a 21st century Sherwood is on the model-shop shelves today. The only aspect of the RTR trains I don't think I could live with are the tension-lock couplers, which sock you in the eye somewhat. With passenger trains as fixed rakes, an auto-coupler is only needed at each end or on 'strengthening' vehicles; the rest can be simple Pendon-type hooks between vehicles. Kadees work well in this context. Freight stock, too, could be made up of 'cuts' of wagons using three-links. In fact, I think you could use three links throughout for goods working - the freight yard, the only location calling for shunting, has good access, and having loose-coupled freights that are loose-coupled seems somehow in keeping with the Sherwood spirit, which was always a bit 'hands on'. At least you won't have to keep winding the engines up!

Summary:
Subject: LMS East Midlands c1937.
Scale/gauge: 4mm/00.
Site size: 16 x 9 ft single garage.
Ruling curve radius: 30ins (loco yard lead). Main lines are 36".
Ruling grade: 1 in 36.
Longest fiddleyard road: c 12 feet.

Further reading:
The 'Sherwood' articles, which appeared in the Railway Modeller between the early 1950s and the late 1980s.

Wickham Market
The GE East Suffolk line in 4mm

One's favourite bits of prototype main line are not always the most modellogenic of subjects, especially where space is limited. This is especially true of many of the lines in East Anglia, where the open and relatively gentle nature of the terrain permits alignments that are, on the whole, best described as 'easy'. Curves there are, certainly, but usually of the mildest variety. Gradients can be quite steep, but they are never very long, often only a few tens of yards. Mountainous it ain't. There was also an unhelpful predilection for station layouts that sprawled lengthways by an unconscionable amount, staggered platforms either side of a level crossing being quite the usual thing. To model many such East Anglian prototype locations, you need a site with plenty of length, a luxury few of us can command.

As you'll have gathered from the introductory chapters, the old GE East Suffolk line was a happy hunting-ground of my youth, and a layout based on some favourite location on the route - Woodbridge, Wickham Market, Saxmundham or Beccles - has long featured in my 'one day' list. Well, unless something very radical happens to the domestic arrangements in my declining years, that day is as far off as ever, as the sites available for my own layouts seem to get shorter, not longer! So I stick with my convoluted bits of Cornwall and assuage my East Anglian thirst by dabbling in branchlines and light railways from those parts. However, my old friend and sparring-partner, John Chambers, is not quite so constrained, and it has long seemed to me that it might - just! - be possible to squeeze a not-too-unbelievable East Suffolk layout into his 17 x 11 foot attic, the largest space I'm contemplating in the context of this book. This somewhat truncated version of Wickham Market is my attempt to do so.

John models in P4, so I have had to take into account the demands of the finer scale standards in coming up with this scheme. Even so, the main line curvatures on the 'offstage' parts of the layout are, at 3ft 6ins, about the minimum you can get away with on a main line P4 layout. They would be fine in EM, and could be reduced to 3ft or a bit under in 00.

The locomotives used on this route in the chosen era - the mid-to-late1950s - ran from Britannia Pacifics through B17, B1, B2 and B12 4-6-0s to K3 moguls, J39s, L1 2-6-4Ts and a range of ex-GE types such as the D16 'Claud Hamilton' 4-4-0s and the common goods classes - J15, J17, J19 and J20. Although most freight workings were hauled by these six-coupled goods engines, this isn't a lot of consolation when you realise that a J20 had a coupled wheelbase of 19ft 6ins - only two feet shorter than a 9F! The WD and ex-GN '01' 2-8-0s could also show from time to time.

Wickham Market advertised itself as the 'junction for the Framlingham branch'. This was a tad misleading, as the actual junction was a mile or so north - at Wickham Market Junction, no less, a great train-watching spot in pleasantly rural surroundings. By the time I knew the East Suffolk line - c1960 - the Framlingham line was reduced to but a daily freight, passenger services having ceased as long ago as the Coronation year. This is an inconvenient fact which Chambers and I have voted unanimously to ignore in the context of this plan, as the antics of the branch passenger trains at Wickham Market were decidedly entertaining.

Wickham Market station (which is, of course, not at Wickham Market at all, but a good country mile away in Campsea Ashe) has one enormous plus from the layout-designing point of view, and that is the skewed-span overbridge by which the B1078 crosses the line at the end of the 'down' platform. This convenient Godsend - a great rarity on a line dominated by level crossings - enables one to vanish the main line 'offstage' at just the right point to hide an extremely inconvenient and most unprototypical curve. Equally fortuitously, the route does curve (gently) in the right direction at the southern end, although my version bends with rather more vigour and starts doing so rather sooner than the original. Wickham Market has some other plus points as a subject; both platforms are relatively short (the 'up' island was uncommonly low as well) and the goods shed is situated opposite the up platform - a relatively compact arrangement. It also has an interesting and very modellable track plan.

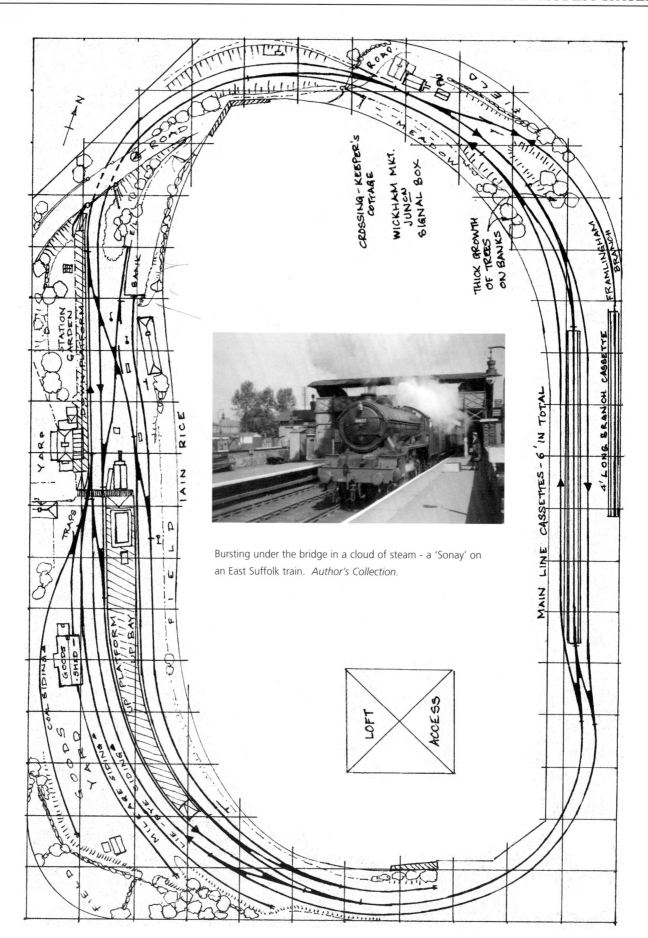

N

ROAD

ROAD

MEADOW

CROSSING-KEEPER'S COTTAGE

WICKHAM MKT. JUNCN SIGNAL BOX

THICK GROWTH OF TREES ON BANKS

FRAMLINGHAM BRANCH

STATION GARDEN

BANK

DOWN PLATFORM

YARD

MAIN LINE RICE

FIELD

TRAPS

GOODS SHED

COAL SIDINGS

GOODS YARD

UP PLATFORM

UP BAY

MILE-PRE SIDING

LIE-PRE SIDING

FIELD

MAIN LINE CASSETTES - 6' IN TOTAL

4' LONG BRANCH CASSETTE

Bursting under the bridge in a cloud of steam - a 'Sonay' on an East Suffolk train. *Author's Collection.*

LOFT ACCESS

Although the main line trains loaded to 8 or even 10 coaches (double headed), locals were usually 3, although often still behind a 4-6-0.

As befitted a station serving a market town, Wickham Market had quite extensive facilities for handling livestock and agricultural implements, including a large loading bank with two end-load ramps on the 'up' side - a favourite vantage point for us pimply youths. A further unusual feature was the short terrace of railway cottages that stood immediately alongside the siding serving the bank. Two of these were unoccupied in my day, but the third housed - if I recall aright - one of the signalmen. The main advantage of the loading bank (as opposed to the bridge - the other natural vantage point) was that it was a lot closer to the signalbox, and you could easily hear the bells as trains were offered forward. The effect when up expresses burst from under the bridge at speed - whistle shrieking amid a cloud of smoke and steam - was splendidly dramatic. You were also well out of harm's way, so Authority usually turned a blind eye so long as you behaved yourself.

Wickham mini-Market

This is very much a display layout, and has been designed so that it functions either as a home layout - viewed from inside - or as an exhibition model, seen from outside. In these circumstances, backdrops are always a problem; my usual solution is a simple neutral sky-blue/grey backdrop on the wall at home, and a portable roll-up drop for exhibition use, erected as a screen behind the model. In either case, presentation uses view-block 'wings' to frame the modelled scene and to cut off that which should not be seen. In an exhibition context, this is a layout that really only has one 'frontage' - not usually a problem as most exhibitions have 'mid block' sites suited to such a format.

As well as the main line and local Ipswich - Beccles passenger trains, local pick-up and through freights and the 'stock trains', the other entertainment Wickham Market was provided by the branch trains from Framlingham. These had, alas, ceased before my time, but I understand the rigmarole went thus: the up Framlingham train came onto the up main line at Wickham Market Junction and puffed serenely into the station from the north - and carried straight on through the up main platform, to the consternation of any passengers who weren't familiar with the proceedings. The train then stopped between the up starter and up advanced starter before setting back into the up bay platform. There was, you see, no facing connection between the up main and up bay platforms. The relieved passengers could then alight - by means of steps placed by the porter - onto the low island platform. Here, they might then have to wait for several minutes to allow main-line trains to pass, Wickham being without a footbridge and all access to the down/bay platforms being by means of a foot crossing.

In the down direction, things were a deal more straightforward. Although it was perfectly possible to run from the up bay onto the down main line via the diamond and trailing turnout between the signalbox and road bridge, this was not the normal route of departure. Or rather, it was - but the train - as if to make up for the mayhem of its arrival - then set back into the down main platform to perform station duties. So the unknowing made their perilous way to the bay to board the train, while canny locals took their ease on the down platform and waited for it to come to them. One likes to think this manoeuvre was staged for the benefit of these passengers, but actually the visit to the down main platform was to ease the work of the station staff in the handling of mail, parcels and so on.

The only other feature of note in the design if this layout is the fiddleyard, which combines through continuous running in both directions with a double-ended cassette system set between the running lines, and linked to both directions. The length of the cassette track is 72ins - long enough for the local workings but not for a full-length express, at least in one bite. The idea is that the 72ins of cassettes are made up of several smaller modules, say, two 30-inch train cassettes and a 12-inch loco cassette. These can be arranged and moved in any order, so an 8-coach train could be handled 'six and two'. Yes, I realise that this isn't very convenient and that maybe a traverser would be better. But in the context of the site, there's not enough width to permit a worthwhile number of traversing tracks while still maintaining adequate curve radii for P4. This compromise is, if you like, the price of finescale. On a wider site, or perhaps for exhibition working, an alternative fiddleyard arrangement using a 6ft (or longer) traverser would be advantageous.

Summary:
Subject: BR (E) GE Section, 1950s.
Scale/gauge: 4mm/P4 (could be 00 or EM).
Site size: 17 x 11 feet.
Ruling curve radius: 42".
Ruling grade: flat.
Longest fiddleyard road: 54".

Further reading:
The main source of inspiration for East Anglian modellers is the series of superb picture albums from the photographs of the late Dr Ian C Allen:
East Anglian Branch Line Album, East Anglian Album, and 55 Years of East Anglian Steam, all published by OPC, and 'Doctor on the Line', published by Irwell Press. Wickham Market and Wickham Market Junction feature widely.

The other useful picture series is East Anglian Steam Gallery, complied by J D Mann and published by South Anglia Productions.

For hard facts:
The Great Eastern railway, by C J Allen. Ian Allan, 1955.
Railway History in Pictures - East Anglia by P. W Swinger, D & C 1983.
Great Eastern Since 1900, by Charles Phillips. Ian Allan, 1985.

Atlantic
PUBLISHERS

Railway Books & Magazines

Modelling & Prototype

Latest catalogue from

ATLANTIC PUBLISHERS

TREVITHICK HOUSE, WEST END, PENRYN, CORNWALL TR10 8HE, UK
Tel: 01326 373656 – Fax: 01326 378309 – E-mail: tr@atlanticpublishers.com

www.AtlanticPublishers.com